SACRED
MOMENTS

SACRED MOMENTS

Tales from the Jewish Life Cycle

selected and edited by
Ronald H. Isaacs and Kerry M. Olitzky

JASON ARONSON INC.
Northvale, New Jersey
London

The authors gratefully acknowledge permission for use of the following material:

"The Right *Yichus*" by Marcia Posner, copyright © 1993 by Marcia Posner. Used by permission of the author.

"The Wedding Blessing," from *Jewish Stories One Generation Tells Another*, retold by Peninnah Schram. Copyright © 1993, 1987 by Peninnah Schram. Published by Jason Aronson Inc. Used by permission of the publisher.

This book was set in 12 pt. Berkeley Old Style by Alpha Graphics of Pittsfield, New Hampshire, and printed by Haddon Craftsmen in Scranton, Pennsylvania.

Library of Congress Cataloging-in-Publication Data

Sacred moments: tales from the Jewish life cycle / selected and edited by Ronald H. Isaacs and Kerry M. Olitzky.
    p. cm.
  ISBN 1-56821-282-8
  1. Legends, Jewish. 2. Tales. 3. Midrash. 4. Life cycle, Human—Religious aspects–Judaism–Legends. I. Isaacs, Ronald H.
  II. Olitzky, Kerry M.
  BM530.S23 1995
  296.1′4–dc20   94-18553

Manufactured in the United States of America. Jason Aronson Inc. offers books and cassettes. For information and catalog write to Jason Aronson Inc., 230 Livingston Street, Northvale, New Jersey 07647.

To the memory of
Barbara and Gene Cohen

Contents

II The Growing Years

III The Middle Years

IV The Older Years

V The Final Years

Preface

The collecting of stories in Jewish tradition is endless. Thus, any collection—regardless of its size—is incomplete. *Sacred Moments: Tales from the Jewish Life Cycle* is a collection of stories concerning the Jewish life cycle; there can never be *the* one definitive collection. Even as you are reading these words, some new story is being shared—parent to child, teacher to student, friend to friend.

Few stories begin in written form. They begin in the context of real living. As a result, stories are fluid in nature. Perhaps that's one of the things that draws us to them as a form. They are not supposed to be exactly the same each time they are told. Each time a story is told, it is really a different story. Details change, if only slightly. Nuances are added. Characters emerge differently as different choices of words are made. One story can spawn a dozen more. Thus, there are similar stories that we find in various collections that share common threads but are different nonetheless. Most stories are part of a diverse oral tradition that eventually gets written down by the student, historian, or storyteller who chooses to keep the story alive as he or she heard it.

While Jewish tradition is transmitted through the generations in a variety of ways, the story is perhaps the most powerful form. It is certainly one of the most effective means of communicating the essential values of our people. In that sense, it is an influential educational vehicle that may be found in a variety of formal and informal settings. Consequently, you may read these stories for your enjoyment, or you can share them with your children and friends. Use them in the classroom or during life-cycle ceremonies. Just keep them alive—for they have kept our people alive as we have traveled throughout history. We invite you to add to this collection. Allow it to grow as you do.

Acknowledgments

The *Kaddish DeRabbanan* (literally, "the Rabbi's *Kaddish*") is said in memory of those teachers who have come before us. It is generally said after the conclusion of study. When we speak these words of memorial, we are mindfully aware that we are links in a *shalshelet hakabbalah*, a chain of tradition, that stretches for generations before us and, please God, after us as well. Thus, through our labors, we are simply fulfilling our obligation to forge the links in that chain we have come to love so dearly.

As songwriter Debbie Friedman has eloquently phrased it in her musical adaptation of the *Kaddish DeRabbanan*, we offer this collection of stories "for our teachers and their students and the students of their students," in memory of all those who taught them in generations past so that we may come to learn and share them with those who are willing to listen. We have become their *Kaddish*.

Ages of a Person

Background: In this statement found in *Pirke Avot* Rabbi Tema suggests various ages for typical milestones in a person's life. While in the modern world, we may disagree, this statement is considered the locus classicus for the Jewish perspective on the life cycle. Thus, it serves as an introduction for all that follows.

At five years of age, [one is ready for] the study of the Bible.

At age ten, [one is prepared for] study of the Mishnah.

At thirteen, [one is] subject to the [responsibility of the] *mitzvot*.

At fifteen, [one is prepared for] study of Talmud.

At eighteen, [one is ready for] marriage.

At twenty, [one should look to] the pursuit of a livelihood.

At thirty, [one is at] the peak of strength.

At forty, [one gains] wisdom.

At fifty, [one is] able to counsel.

At sixty, old age creeps in.

At seventy, [one gains] fullness of years.

At eighty, [one reaches] the age of strength.

At ninety, the body is bent.

At a hundred, [one is] as good as dead and completely out of this world.

Pirke Avot 5:24

I
THE
BEGINNING
YEARS

The *mitzvah* of being fruitful and multiplying exists so that the earth will be settled. And it is a great *mitzvah* . . . because of it, all others exist.

Sefer Hachinuch, Bereshit

The Jewish people has been called the people of the book, but we are just as surely the people of the family. Our people began centuries ago as the family of Abraham and Sarah, Isaac and Rebecca, and Jacob and Leah and Rachel. They have remained with us across the miles, across the years. In reading their stories, we become part of them, as they become part of us. Since that time of the origin of our people, amidst triumph and tribulation, our family has grown. Sometimes, our ability to survive in hostile environments has surpassed human understanding. One thing remains clear: our strategy for survival has included—perhaps above all else—the transmission of Judaism through our children in the context of family, whatever shape that family has taken. No school can match the influence of the family in the education it can provide its members.

There are lots of different paths to becoming a Jewish family, but we have to begin somewhere. Most of us were either born into a Jewish family or made a conscious

decision to join one as adults. But actually building a Jewish family is a privilege that involves hard work. With it
comes responsibility. Family doesn't come easy. Becoming
a family by bringing a child into the world is one of the
wondrous miracles of life itself. To sanctify this moment,
throughout our history, we have created a rich variety of
rites and ceremonies, guided by rules and procedures for
the beginning years of Jewish life. All the while, religious
creativity has constantly enhanced these ceremonies.
Whether these ceremonies have survived has been a test
of creative religious genius. Therefore, we have a vast collection of stories related to creation, birth, and the covenant of circumcision (*brit milah*) that have been passed
down through the centuries. In this section of *Tales from
the Jewish Life Cycle*, we include selections from that rich
treasure house of stories specifically related to the themes
of conception and birth, the creation of souls, and tales
related to circumcision, one of the early acts of faith that
affirms God's covenantal relationship with the Jewish
people.

Creation

Hillel and Shammai Argue about the Creation of Humans

Background: This talmudic story presents one of many arguments between the two important schools of thought— Hillel and Shammai. The topic of this argument concerns the creation of the human species and whether it might have been better for God not to have created human beings since we are prone to err and to sin.

For two and one-half years the schools of Hillel and Shammai argued with each other. Shammai argued and said, "It would have been better for humans not to have been created than to have been created." Hillel retorted, "It is better that humans have been created than it would have been had we not been created." They finally voted and this is what was decided: "It would have been better for humans not to have been created than to have been created. However, now that humans do exist, let us search our past deeds and attempt to carefully examine what we are about to do."

Babylonian Talmud, *Eruvin* 13b

Birth of Humans

Background: This talmudic story provides us with some ancient insights into the nature of the human species itself.

Rabbi Simon said, "When God came to create the first human, the ministering angels divided into several factions. One group of angels said, "Let Adam not be created." Another said, "Let Adam be created."

Mercy said, "Let Adam be created, for humans will be merciful."

Truth said, "Let Adam not be created, for humans will always be telling lies."

Righteousness said, "Let Adam be created, for humans will do righteous things."

Peace said, "Let humans not be created, for they are all contention."

So what did God do? God took Truth and flung Truth to the earth.

The ministering angels then said to God, "Why do You disgrace Your own seal? Raise Truth from the earth."

Rabbi Huna said, "While the ministering angels were still arguing and disputing, God created Adam. Then God said to the angels, "Why do you still argue? The first human is already made."

Tanchuma, Genesis 2:4

Adam Is Born

Background: According to the Bible, Adam, the first human, was created by God on the sixth day. This story is an attempt to explain why God waited until day six before creating humans.

A question was once asked: Why was Adam, the first human, created on the sixth day of creation? Would it not have been better to create this very important person on the first day, to show the great importance of the human species?

The tradition gives several reasons for Adam's creation on the sixth day. One opinion is that God waited until the sixth day to create Adam to show that individuals should not grow so arrogant as to boast, "See how great I am!" If anyone should ever say this, it would be quickly shown that even tiny insects were created before humans.

Another answer is given by the tradition for the creation of Adam on the sixth day. God wanted Adam to be immediately able to participate in the celebration of the Sabbath and enjoy the Sabbath meal.

This answer is similar to a king who built a magnificent palace and prepared a very spectacular meal in it. It was only then that the king invited the guests to come and partake. Similarly in the case of Adam, it was only when all of creation was finished that God felt it was the proper time to invite the honored guests into the world.

Various traditional sources

Deciding on a Path

Background: When a child enters the world, what forces are at play that direct the child? Will she or he follow the good path or will she or he live a life of sin? This story offers us insight into the mysteries of life between conception and birth.

The soul and body of a human being are united in the following manner: After a man and woman have made love and the woman has conceived, the Angel of the Night, Lilah, carries the sperm before God. God then decides what shall be the distinguishing characteristics of that child—whether the child shall be male or female, strong or weak, rich or poor, beautiful or ugly, long or short, fat or thin. Piety and wickedness, however, are left to the determination of the individual.

Then God signals the angel who has been given the charge to watch over that particular soul. God says, "Bring Me the soul of this child whose form is hidden in Paradise." The angel brings the designated soul. At that moment, God issues the command for the soul to enter the sperm. Yet the soul pleads, "*Ribbono shel Olam.* I am well pleased with *this* world, the world in which I have been living since You have called me forth into being. Why do You suddenly want me to enter into this sperm, I who am pure and filled with divine glory?" God consoles her by saying, "The world I shall cause you to enter is better than the world in which you have been living. When I created you, it was only for this purpose." The soul is then forced to enter the sperm and the angel carries her back to the womb of her mother. Two angels are dispatched to watch

over the soul so that she will not leave it or drop out of it.
A light is set above her so that the soul can see from one
end of the world to the other.

In the morning, the angel carries the soul to Paradise
and shows her the righteous who sit in glory with crowns
upon their heads. The angel then says to the soul, "Do you
know where you are? These whom you behold here were
formed, like you, in the womb of their mother. When they
came into this world, they observed God's Torah and followed God's *mitzvot*. They were good, decent people. As
partners with their Creator, following their body's death,
they now enjoy this Paradise. Know also that you will one
day depart this world. If you only observe God's Torah you
too will eventually sit with them. If not, you will be doomed
to sit in the other place."

In the evening, the angel takes the soul to hell and
there points out the sinners whom the Angel of Destruction is taunting with fire. During the visit, the soul hears
the sinners crying out in the black night, "Woe! Woe!" but
no mercy is shown to them. The angel then asks the same
question that was asked before: "Do you know who these
people are? They are now consumed with fire but they were
created just like you. When they were sent out into the
world, they forgot their origins; they did not observe God's
Torah and *mitzvot*. Therefore they have to come to the disgrace they now suffer. Know that your destiny is also to
depart from this world. Be just, therefore, and not wicked,
so that you may gain entrance to a future world."

Between morning and evening the angel carries the
soul around and shows her where she will lie and where
she will die, and the place that she will be buried. The angel
takes her on a tour of the entire world. In the evening, the
angel places the soul in the womb of the mother, and there

she remains for nine months. During this time, the angel assigned to the soul teaches Torah to the babe. When the time arrives for her to emerge from the womb into the world, the soul is reluctant to leave. She has enjoyed the warmth of the womb and the light of Torah. So the angel touches the babe above the lip and sends it forth into the world. Immediately the child forgets all it had seen and comes into the world crying, yearning for the Torah it now does not realize it has lost.

Based on Tanchuma, *Pekudei*

The Soul

How a Person Gets a Soul

Background: According to Jewish tradition a person consists of both a body and a soul. This story attempts to explain the origin of the soul.

Before the formation of a child in its mother's womb, God is approached by the angel who is in charge of giving birth, with a drop of semen in its hand.

"O God," the angel says, "the soul that will be put here, what is it to be?"

And God then decrees whether the child to be born is to be a male or female, weak or strong, tall or short, thin or fat. By way of a decree, God then announces all that will happen to that child.

There is only one thing that God does not decide, and that is whether the child will be good or evil. That alone is for the child to decide.

Following this procedure, God calls to the angel who is appointed over the various souls in the heavens and says, "Bring Me such and such a soul who will be found in *Gan Eden*."

When that soul is brought before God, it bows before God and God says, "I wish you to enter this drop so that you will leave this world and enter the world of people."

Immediately the soul protests and says, "O God of the universe, I am more than happy with the world in which I find myself today. Here I am pure and formed in Your image. Why do You want me to enter this semen drop and become part of a physical and mortal body?"

Notwithstanding the complaint, the soul does indeed enter the drop and it is placed into the mother's womb. There, two angels guard it from any harm and it is able to see all that takes place throughout the world. The soul sees righteous people sitting with crowns on their heads in the Garden of Eden. The angel explains that these were placed in the world and always observed the Torah and the *mitzvot* with great care. Because of this, they were rewarded with the Garden of Eden. "You too," says the angel to the soul, "will be rewarded if you observe God's laws."

The next night, the angel shows the soul the terrors of the netherworld and explains to the soul that people down in the netherworld were violators of the *mitzvot*.

The angel then says to the soul, "The choice is yours. It is in your hands either to observe the Torah or to violate it and suffer the punishment of the netherworld."

Thus the angel teaches the little soul—both the righteous and evil live in the world. Having seen all of this, the soul rests within her mother for nine months. Toward the end of this time, the angel approaches the little soul and says, "Your time has now come to go out into the air of the outside world."

"Why must I go?" protests the soul.

"You must listen to me," answers the angel. "There is no choice in this matter. Despite yourself you were created, and despite yourself you will eventually die."

Crying in protest, the little soul refuses to leave. Finally the angel drags her out. That is why the child cries for so long when it comes into the outside world. Immediately upon going into the world, however, it forgets about all that had previously happened.

In the final moments of any person's life, the same angel comes to that person and asks, "Do you recognize me?"

"Yes," comes the reply, "but why do you come to me on this particular day?"

"I come," replied the angel, "because it is time for you to leave this world. It's the hour of your death."

But the person cries out, "I do not want to die! Allow me to stay where I am."

But the angel shakes its head and sadly reports, "Do you remember that I told you when you were still very young that in spite of yourself you were created by God and in spite of yourself you must also die? Now is the time for the final thing that I said, and now you must give an accounting of your deeds in this world before God the Almighty One."

And so a person is born and dies. At birth a person knows what she must do. In her lifetime she knows what she must accomplish. The rest is up to the person.

Various traditional sources

Soul Meets Body

Background: This story offers us a view of the prenatal state of the child. While the folklore of other peoples includes birth stories, Jewish folklore focuses on this prenatal stage because the soul is said to exist prior to the birth of the child.

The angel that has presided over souls since the beginning of time is summoned by God to bring a soul each time a child is to be born. The angel decides whether the child should be strong or weak, male or female. However, the decision as to whether the child should be just or wicked is left to the free will of the individual. Just when the soul is ready to enter the body of the child to be born, the soul appears before God and implores God to be allowed to remain in heaven.

"I am happy here, where I am holy and pure, and would rather not enter into that vile matter."

"You are being sent into the world," replies God, "where it is better than where you have been dwelling. It is for that purpose that you were created."

And so the soul, against its own inclination, is introduced into the body. And two angels lead the child into Paradise, where it is allowed to see the souls of the just who during their life's journey on earth had obeyed God's *mitzvot* and had been just. Then the soul is taken to hell, where it is allowed to observe the tortures of the souls of the wicked. It is also taken to places where it is destined to dwell. When the moment of birth arrives, the soul once more pleads and begs to remain. But the Angel of Birth replies that the soul must go out into the world even if it is against its will. And immediately the child begins to cry, but the angel slaps it on the nose and it forgets all that it had known in its prenatal state.

Based on *Seder Yetzirat Havlad*

Lilith's Mission

Background: Of the many myths surrounding Lilith, many implicate her in jeopardizing the life of babies. Therefore, various amulets are prepared to ward off both Lilith and the Angel of Death. Often they take the simple form of a sheet of paper with the words from Psalm 121 printed on it and placed in the room of a woman in childbirth. Under the psalm, other words are written to ward off Lilith. Often a *magen David* is also drawn.

Lilith, like Adam, was created from the dust of the earth (*adamah*) and presented to Adam as a partner. As soon as Lilith joined Adam, they began to quarrel. Neither wanted to be submissive or subservient to the other. "I am your lord and master," shouted Adam, "and it is your obligation to obey me." But Lilith was not so easily mastered. In a mocking tone, she replied, "Are we not equals? Have we not both been created from dust? I will not be submissive to you." They continued to quarrel and neither would give up his or her autonomy. At last, weary of living with her partner, Lilith voiced the name of God (YHWH) and fled, soaring up to the celestial regions. In his distress, Adam addressed himself to his Creator: "Lord God, the woman you have sent me has fled from me." In response, God sent three angels, commanding them to seize Lilith and return her to Adam. If she refused to return with them, they were told to tell her that any of her offspring would die.

The angels followed Lilith and found her in the midst of the sea, struggling with mighty waves. When they communicated God's directive to her, she refused and an-

swered, "Don't you know that I was created for the purpose of weakening and punishing little children, infants
and babies? I have power over them from the day they are
born until the eighth day, if they are boys, and until the
twentieth day, if they are girls."

When the angels heard what Lilith had to say, they
wanted to forcefully drown her, but she begged them to
let her live. However, she had to swear to them in the name
of the living God that if she saw their names (Sanui,
Sansanui, and S'mangaluf) in the presence of a newborn
child she would leave immediately without hurting the
baby. But because she had refused to return to Adam, every
day one hundred of her own children (demons) would die.

Based on a myth from *Sefer Ben Sirach* (see also Babylonian
Talmud, *Eruvin* 18b)

Creating a Soul

Background: While mother and father are integral partners in conception, Judaism holds that God also participates in this life-giving event. This story explains God's role in the process of procreation.

The Holy Blessed One said, "My *Shechinah* and I are partners in the creation of the soul. The child's father and mother are partners in the creation of the body. The child's father issues the seed for the design of the whites of the eyes, bones, sinews, and brains while the woman offers the black of the eyes, hair, flesh, and skin. Likewise, the heaven and the earth and all their hosts participate in creation. From the angels come the good and evil inclination so that the human is assembled from both. The sun and the moon offer the child light by day and night. Animals, birds, and fish provide nourishment, as do the trees and seeds of the earth. What did the Holy Blessed One do? God uprooted Adam and Eve from the Garden of Eden and took them to be with God in the joy of their children. There is no joy like the joy of redemption as it is written: "Let the heavens be glad. Let the earth rejoice. Let them say among the nations, '*Adonai* reigns'" (Chronicles 16:31).

Based on *Zohar* III, 119b–120a

Serving Water in Chelm

Background: Jewish tradition is filled with wonderfully silly stories of the "wise men of Chelm," a fictional village in Europe. The citizens of this community display a lack of logic that often reveals a great deal of profound insight and wisdom for daily living.

Many of the most important citizens of Chelm gathered to celebrate the *brit milah* of Reb Yossel's first son. The tables were covered with fine linen. On each table was sparkling stemware. But, as far as food and drink was concerned, only jugs of water occupied prime spots on each table. After a while, it became apparent that water was all that was to be served.

People asked Reb Yossel, "What is the big idea of inviting all of these people and serving only water?"

Reb Yossel replied, "Water is the very best thing I could serve. You see, yesterday I went to the market to buy some fish to serve today to my guests. I told the fishmonger that I wanted to buy the very best. He told me, 'This is the very best. The fish are sweet like sugar.'

"I figured that sugar must be better than fish. So I decided to buy sugar instead. When I went to the store to buy the sugar, the storekeeper told me, 'This sugar is as sweet as honey.'

"I decided that honey must be better than sugar, so I asked the storekeeper if he had honey for sale. He replied, 'I have honey that is as pure as oil.' 'In that case,' I told him, 'let me purchase some oil.' To that request, he replied, 'My oil is as pure as water.'

"If that were the case, I reasoned, sugar better than fish, honey better than sugar, oil better than honey, and water better than oil, then isn't water the best thing I could buy for my guests? I certainly would not think of giving my guests, those who come to honor me for my first son's *brit milah*, anything but the best!"

Various traditional sources

Chana's Struggle

Background: While we know the story of Chana and her struggle with conception, we do not know exactly what took place during the encounter at the *mishkan* at Shiloh. In the general tradition of *midrash*, this tale attempts to fill in the details.

In the Bible, during the period of the judges, Elkanah and his two wives, Peninah and Chana, went up to the *mishkan* in Shiloh in order to observe Rosh Hashanah. On the day of the festival, they sat down to their meal with elevated spirits.

Peninah thought to herself, "God has really blessed me. I have a righteous spouse and healthy children. I thank God for all that He has given to me." Chana was not so happy. She felt alone in her childlessness. She felt forsaken. Particularly at this time of year, she felt her pain ever so acutely.

Chana thought to herself, "Dear God, when will You bless me as You have Peninah? Will I ever be able to embrace my own children and hold them close to me? I have waited many years for a child, but I am still alone." Sensing Chana's distress, Elkanah tried to cheer her up, but instead she was moved to tears. "What is troubling you, Chana?" he queried. Chana was too upset to even attempt to answer.

After dinner, Chana opened her heart and soul to God in prayer. Her prayer of silence emanated from the very depths of her being. Her lips moved, but her voice could not be heard. "Creator of the world, You have made so many creatures, large and small. Could You not make just one more? How much I long for a child to grow and be able to serve You. If You bless me with a child, I swear I will bring that child to this sanctuary and consecrate him to You. Please give me a child."

Eli, the high priest, noticed Chana. "What kind of woman is this?" he mused to himself. "She moves her lips, yet her eyes are tightly closed. Others speak their words of prayer aloud so that their words can be heard. Perhaps she is drunk or mentally disturbed. Does she even know what she is doing? Perhaps I should chase her away so that she does not defile this holy place of sanctuary?"

Eli approached the woman and upbraided her for her drunken behavior. Chana replied, "I am not drunk. I am bitter because I suffer. I have come here to pour out my heart to God."

Humbled by Chana's sincerity, he blessed her and sent her on her way. That same year, Chana conceived and bore a child.

Based on Babylonian Talmud, *Berachot* 31a

The Child Born
Out of Wedlock

Background: This talmudic story deals with the attempt to ascertain which of two sons of a particular woman was born out of wedlock. Once again, we see the important use of dreams in solving this enigma.

Once a man overheard his wife say that one of her two sons was the child of a lover. The husband was deeply distressed. Filled with anguish, he took ill. Before the man died, he shared the saga of his wife's infidelity with all of his friends and asked that his property be given to his own son.

The man's friends, not knowing what to do, went to Rabbi Banaah and asked for his guidance. The rabbi said, "Let the two sons take canes and beat upon the grave of their father until he appears to them in a dream and tells them which is truly his own son."

The real son refused to dishonor the grave of his father but the other son was willing to do so. As a result, Rabbi Banaah gave the property to the son who had protested against the desecration of his father's grave.

Babylonian Talmud, *Bava Batra* 58a

Circumcision

The Greediest Mohel

Background: This folktale expresses the important Jewish value of giving *tzedakah*.

Once there was a *mohel* (the one who performs the ritual circumcision) who was so greedy that he was called the *kamzan*—"the tongs"—because he never gave away any of his gold. Each day he would spend several hours in front of his vault staring at his money in delight. Yet he always believed that he was a kind and righteous man, because he would never charge a poor person for a circumcision.

One day a stranger came and asked him to perform a circumcision. Seeing that the man was wealthy, the *kamzan* was very eager to go. At long last they reached a huge mansion, and the *kamzan* entered the house. He was greeted by the little child's mother, who said, "Be careful, my friend, for my husband is a spirit. Do not eat or drink anything while you are here, and absolutely do not accept any gifts."

They came into a large room where the host offered the *kamzan* food to eat. The *kamzan* refused and desired to return to his home.

Next they came to a room filled with many silver objects. The host told the *mohel* to choose anything his heart desired, but he refused.

Finally, the host brought the *kamzan* into an empty room where many keys were hanging on the wall. The *kamzan* immediately recognized that one of the keys was to his own vault.

As if reading his mind, the host said, "Yes, *kamzan*, it is your key." By now the *mohel* became very frightened. His host said to him, "When a person purchases a vault, two keys are made. One is for the person and the other for God. If God's key is not used, we keep it here. A person is not the master of his own money and if he keeps putting money in but never takes any out to give away, then his soul is locked inside the vault."

The *kamzan* shuddered in fear and now realized that the spirit to whom he was speaking was the Angel of Death!

The spirit then said, "Remember all that you have seen here today. There will be no second chances. Now take God's key and return to your home, so you can be the master of your own money."

From that day on the *mohel*'s hand was always open to the needy and poor, and nobody ever again called him *kamzan*.

Jewish folktale

The Circumcision of Rabbi Judah the Patriarch

Background: This story describes a time during the period of Roman rule when Israelites were forbidden to circumcise their children. The story goes on to describe how Rabbi Judah the Patriarch and Marcus Aurelius (surnamed Antoninus in this story), the emperor of Rome, became friends.

A long time ago the Roman government issued a decree prohibiting Israel from circumcising their children. During that period, Rabbi Judah the Patriarch was born. His father, Rabban Simeon ben Gamaliel, asked, "How dare we forsake the decree of our Holy One and comply with the decree of the wicked ones?" Immediately, he rose up and circumcised his son.

When the city magistrate heard what had happened, he had Rabban Simeon ben Gamaliel summoned. He asked him, "Why did you violate the decree of the emperor?" Rabbi Simeon answered, "We are only doing what our God has commanded us." The magistrate replied, "I do respect you since you are the head of your people, but I cannot allow you to violate our emperor's wishes."

The magistrate then sent Rabbi Judah the Patriarch and his mother to the emperor for his decree. Traveling all day, they finally arrived at the inn kept by the grandfather of Antoninus. And as it happened, Antoninus was born at the very time that Rabbi Judah the Patriarch was born.

Rabbi Judah's mother was held in affection by Antoninus' mother, so she went to see her at once. When they met, Antoninus' mother asked, "What troubles you?" Rabbi Judah's mother answered, "We were told by the emperor that we could not circumcise our son, and since I did circumcise him, we are now to go to the emperor to learn our fate."

Upon hearing this, Antoninus' mother replied, "If you desire, take my child, who is not circumcised, and give me your child." The switch was made, and the mother of Rabbi Judah continued on her journey.

When they arrived at the palace, the emperor commanded that the child be examined. Of course they found him to be uncircumcised. Turning to his magistrate, the emperor screamed aloud, "My decree concerned circumcised children, and you brought me an uncircumcised one!" The magistrate was then put to death, and the mother and rabbi were sent away in peace.

When the two returned to the house of Antoninus, his mother said, "Since God has brought a miracle for you through me and for your son through my son, let them be friends forever!"

Bet Hamidrash, ed. A. Jellinek

The Mark of Completion

Background: This midrashic story explains that individuals are born incomplete and unfinished. The mark of circumcision provides a young boy with a "finishing touch," so to speak.

A pagan philosopher once asked Rabbi Hoshai, "If circumcision is so dear to God, why was Adam not created with the mark of circumcision?" The rabbi replied, "According to your reasoning, why should a man like you shave the hair on his head but at the same time leave the adult hair of his beard intact?" The pagan replied, "Because the hair of his head grew with him in the days of his foolish childhood."

Rabbi Hoshai then argued, "If so, he should blind his eyes, cut off his hands, and break his legs, which also grew along with him since the days of his foolish childhood."

The pagan philosopher answered, "Have we come down to such folly?" The rabbi replied, "I cannot let you go without a proper answer. You see, everything that was created by God during the six days of creation needs finishing: mustard needs sweetening, vetches need sweetening, wheat needs grinding, and even people need finishing."

Genesis Rabbah 11:6

The Saving Power
of Circumcision

Background: In presenting the importance of the religious commandment of circumcision, this story attempts to show its miraculous power.

A caesar once said to Rabbi Tanchum, "Come, let us all be one people." "Very well," Rabbi Tanchum answered, "but we who are already circumcised cannot possibly go back and become like you. Therefore, you go and circumcise yourselves and become like us."

To this suggestion the caesar replied, "Well spoken! But he who prevails over the emperor is thrown into the wild animal pen." Accordingly, Rabbi Tanchum was thrown into the pen in the arena, but the animals did not eat him! A certain heretic said, "The only reason the animals did not eat him is that they were not hungry." At that, he himself was thrown into the pen, and the animals ate him.

Babylonian Talmud, *Sanhedrin* 39a

The Circumcision of Monobazos and Zotos

Background: This midrashic story explains how the sons of King Ptolemy were circumcised.

Once, Monobazos and Zotos, the two sons of King Ptolemy, sat reading the Book of Genesis. When they reached the verse "And you shall be circumcised in the flesh of your foreskin" (Genesis 17:11), each son turned to the wall and began to cry. Then each went and had himself circumcised.

Time passed, and again they sat together and read from the Book of Genesis. When they reached the verse "And you shall be circumcised," one said to the other, "Alas, my brother." The other replied, "Alas for you, my brother, but not for me." Then each informed the other of what he had done.

When the boys' mother became aware of it, she went and told their father, "Your sons had a growth on their organ and the doctor ordered that they be circumcised." He then said to her, "Then let them be circumcised."

Genesis Rabbah 46:10 and Yalkut, *Lech Lecha* 82

Reb Mordechai of Lechovitch

Background: The rabbinic sages have also stressed the importance of hastening to perform a religious obligation. It is because of this that traditional circumcisions will often be held in the early part of the day. This story is about two circumcisions that were held during the early part of the day.

Reb Mordechai of Lechovitch was a famous *mohel*. He was so eager when presented with an opportunity to perform a circumcision that he never declined an invitation.

One day on the Sabbath of the eve of Chanukah he was presented with the honor of performing two circumcisions in two villages that were very far away from each other. One was in the north and the other in the south. When his disciples heard that he had accepted the invitation to perform two circumcisions in places so far away from each other, they asked him whether he thought he could do this on a wintry day that was so very short.

Reb Mordechai answered, "Regarding a certain passage in the Torah, the Talmud tells us that it comes to teach us of the eagerness of Abraham, which I understand to mean that the Torah *teaches us* Abraham's eagerness. In fact, the Torah *implants* it in us."

And thus Reb Mordechai rose very early in the morning and, hastening with enthusiasm, was able to perform two circumcisions in two villages that were far apart. He came home very tired, but in time to prepare for the holy *Shabbat*.

Chasidic story

An Unblemished Mitzvah

Background: This story reiterates Judaism's reverence for the person who performs a circumcision, for it is such an important *mitzvah*.

One of the young students of Reb Mordechai of Lechovitch was constantly being castigated by his father-in-law, an outstanding scholar and *mitnaged*. "You are just too lazy to study," he would say.

One day a son was born to the young man and his wife. Since he was a devoted *chasid*, he decided to honor his rebbe, Reb Mordechai, with the *mitzvah* of performing the circumcision. The eighth day finally arrived, and the father arose early to say his morning prayers in the synagogue with his rebbe. Meanwhile, the young man's father-in-law had hired another *mohel*. He had the boy circumcised while his son-in-law and Reb Mordechai were still finishing their prayers.

When the young father and his rebbe returned home from synagogue, they were excited about the impending *brit milah*. Upon their arrival, they were shocked to learn that the circumcision had already been completed. The young man was very upset and felt that his rebbe had been slighted as well. But what could he now do? Quietly he went to the rebbe's home for the *seudat mitzvah*, the festive meal.

Imagine the surprise of all the *chasidim* when they witnessed the rebbe happier than they had ever seen him—even when he had in fact not performed the circumcision himself. What could possibly be an explanation for his happiness?

The rebbe explained, "The *mitzvah* of circumcision is one held in high esteem, but it is almost always tainted by the shadow of someone looking for special honor. The rabbis teach us that if an emergency arose that prevented a person from doing a *mitzvah*, the Bible gives that person credit for good intention, as if he had actually performed the *mitzvah*. Obviously, a *mitzvah* such as a circumcision has no ulterior motive and is reckoned by God as having been carried out in the most perfect manner possible. This is why I have reasons to rejoice more than usual. For how often do I get a chance to do a *mitzvah* that is so pure and untainted?"

Chasidic story

Abraham's Circumcision Consolation

Background: According to the Torah, Abraham circumcised himself when he was ninety-nine years of age (Genesis 17:24). This story attempts to explain why he performed his own circumcision.

When God told Abraham to circumcise himself, Abraham decided to consult with three of his friends. Obnor told him that at his age, it was not worth aggravating himself with such a ceremony. Eshkol said, "Abraham, shall you aggravate yourself among all of your enemies?" But Abraham's friend Mamre told him, "God protected you when you were thrown into the fire and helped you with your war against the kings. Surely you shall listen to what God tells you now about your circumcision."

In case one might ask why Abraham, who had once withstood the ten tests that God have given him, would now go and ask for his friends' advice, the answer is a simple one. Abraham never truly intended to leave the decision in the hands of his three friends. He was forever ready to perform God's instruction, but he wanted to test the opinions and character of his friends. He learned that Obnor and Eshkol were not his real friends and that only Mamre shared his faith. This is the reason Abraham performed his own circumcision at the place called "Elonei Mamre."

Adapted from the stories of Rabbi Avraham Chezkoni

Rashi's Circumcision

Background: The figure of the Prophet Elijah is an integral part of the modern-day circumcision ceremony. It was Elijah who complained bitterly when the Jewish people began to forsake the religious obligation of circumcision. This story relates the appearance of Elijah at the circumcision of Rashi, one of the greatest biblical and talmudic scholars ever to have lived.

The story is told that during the night that the great commentator Rashi was born, the Prophet Elijah revealed himself in a dream to his father, telling him to name the newborn son "Shlomo." When the boy was to be circumcised eight days later, he was to wait for Elijah's appearance so that he could be the *sandek*.

On the eighth day, a large group of people gathered in the house of Rabbi Yitzchak. They waited for the *brit milah* to begin, but time passed and nothing happened. Growing impatient, they asked the father the reason for the delay. Maybe something had happened to the mother or the child? The day had almost passed, but the father gave one excuse after another for the delay. It was almost night and the Prophet Elijah had not appeared.

Suddenly, a poor man in tattered clothes appeared at the door. Rabbi Yitzchak immediately recognized him as the man in his dream. He joyously welcomed the guest and invited him to sit on the special chair prepared for the *sandek*. The guests were astonished, but no one asked any questions. They believed that the rabbi had to know what he was doing.

At the end of the *brit milah*, the poor man offered some astonishing words of Torah. When he concluded, he slipped out of the house and disappeared into thin air! Only then did the people realize that he was not an ordinary person but the Prophet Elijah, and that the baby was no ordinary baby but an extraordinary child.

The child was immediately recognized by the world to be unusual, with extraordinary qualities of intelligence and kindness.

Various traditional sources

Abraham's Recovery

Background: This story presents an explanation for the biblical verse from Psalm 82:1: "God always stands in a godly congregation."

When Abraham was recovering from his circumcision at the age of one hundred, God visited him. While God was visiting him, Abraham was seated. Realizing that it was inappropriate to sit in the presence of God, Abraham attempted to stand. God said to Abraham, "Do not overburden yourself. Please remain seated!" But Abraham replied, "O my God, it is not respectful for me to sit while You stand." And God answered again, "Do not overburden yourself, for you are a man of one hundred years. Because you in your old age sit while I stand, your descendants, when they are little children ages three and four, shall sit in synagogues and schools, and I will stand among them. This is because 'God always stands in a godly congregation' [Psalm 82:1]."

Tanchuma, *Vayera* 43b

II
THE
GROWING
YEARS

At thirteen, one is ready to fulfill commandments.

Pirke Avot 5:23

*B*ar and *bat mitzvah*, literally "son" and "daughter" of the commandment, provide us with a focus for what we have called "The Growing Years." Of course, other events take place during these years—in the synagogue, at home, and elsewhere. But the *bar* and *bat mitzvah* become points of transition, moving the child in the direction of adulthood, eventually to leave childhood behind. The *bar* and *bat mitzvah* also reflect the struggle of adolescence, that difficult period we all must somehow survive, as children and as parents.

While the ceremony of *bar* and *bat mitzvah* as we know it is a relatively recent phenomenon, it has come to represent a rite of passage when a Jewish child reaches the age when he or she becomes personally responsible for the performance of *mitzvot*. Parents publicly thank God for being released from the obligation of their children. This often misunderstood blessing really thanks God for allowing the child to reach the age when he or she does not bear the burden of responsibility carried by his or her parents' actions. Finally, the child—now adult—is able to succeed or fail on his or her own merit. In some synagogues, this blessing has been replaced by a ritual fondly called "the Torah transmission" during which grandparents, then parents, take the Torah from the ark and physi-

cally hand down the Torah to the young person marking his *bar mitzvah* or her *bat mitzvah*.

According to traditional Jewish law, a boy reaches this new age of responsibility when he becomes thirteen. For a girl, the age of responsibility comes at twelve. In recent times, this distinction has been equalized in our struggle for reaching equality in most liberal communities. Before the thirteenth or fourteenth century, there was no real ritual that marked this transition into adulthood. It simply occurred.

This section presents several stories related to the themes of coming of age, assuming responsibility, and how the Israelites received the Torah. We invite you to match your experiences with those described in the stories that follow.

Study

Brothers

Background: A certain couple had two sons, one age twelve, the other age ten. The older boy had a sharp mind and excelled in school. He became known in his neighborhood as a child prodigy, for his talmudic learning was both deep and wide. The second son, while very intelligent, seemed pale in comparison to his brother.

As they grew older, the older boy's reputation spread and, as a result, he became rather haughty and overbearing. Sometimes his behavior led him into rather serious altercations that once or twice even ended in fistfights.

The boys' parents were not happy with what had happened to their children. Once, when the father could handle it no longer, he actually spanked the older boy in the presence of the boy's friends and their neighbors. The father had become frustrated and wanted some way to communicate to people that he too disapproved of his own son's behavior. What really bothered this father was that the younger son soon began to follow his older brother's example.

The father called the younger son to him and said, "Listen, you saw what I did to your brother. Even though he has a reputation as a genius, I had no mercy on him. For the disgraceful way he was acting, I embarrassed him in the presence of our family and friends. Figure it out. If you continue, you will get the same and you do not have the reputation of being a genius."

Chafetz Chayyim

Coming of Age

Background: This story demonstrates the importance placed on teaching a child Torah until reaching the age of majority at thirteen years. Until that age, parents are responsible for their children.

Once Rabbi Akiba was meandering through a graveyard when he met a charcoal burner who was carrying wood on his shoulders. Rabbi Akiba was very puzzled and ordered the individual to stop. He said to him, "My son, why are you working so hard? If you are a servant and your master works you too hard, I will redeem you and set you free. If you are poor, I will give you the necessary funds so that you may live!"

The stranger replied, "Leave me alone, for I cannot stay."

Rabbi Akiba asked, "Are you a human being or a demon?"

The man answered, "I am of the dead, and my fate is to carry and gather up wood on a daily basis."

Akiba then asked him, "What was your trade when you were alive?"

The man responded, "I was a tax collector, and I used to favor the rich and antagonize the poor."

Akiba then said, "My son, have you heard from those who are responsible for you that there is any remedy for you?"

The man answered, "For me there is no remedy. Yet, I did hear that the burden of my punishment would be lessened if I had a child who could stand up in the congregation and proclaim publicly, 'Praised be God, who is worthy to be praised.' But alas, I have no child. On my death, I left my wife pregnant, but I don't know whether she gave birth. And if she did give birth, who will teach my child Torah?"

Akiba then asked the stranger, "What is your name and what is your wife's name?"

The man answered him, telling him also the name of the city in which he lived.

Akiba then traveled from city to city until he came to the man's hometown. Akiba asked many people about the man and his family. To Akiba's query, they all responded, "May his bones be ground in hell." Then he asked about his wife and they said, "May her name be blotted out of the world." Then he inquired about their child and they said, "The boy wasn't even circumcised!"

Akiba at once took the child into his own home and began to teach him Torah, but first he fasted for forty days. He taught the young boy the Hebrew alphabet, the *Shema* prayer, the Grace after Meals, and *tefillah*. Then he made the boy stand up in the synagogue and pray, "Praised be God, who is worthy to be praised."

At that moment the charcoal burner's punishment was lifted, and he came to Rabbi Akiba in a dream and said, "May you sleep in Paradise, even as you have rescued me from hell." Akiba replied with the verse "O God, Your Name is forever and Your memorial is for every generation" (Psalm 135:13).

Pirke Derech Eretz, p. 22

The Maturing of Jacob and Esau

Background: This story from the *Midrash* is an attempt to show that parents are relieved of the responsibility for the actions of their children when they reach the age of thirteen.

Rabbi Pinchas said in the name of Rabbi Levi, "Jacob and Esau were like a myrtle and a wild rose bush growing side by side. When they grew up, one yielded its fragrance [i.e., Jacob] while the other [Esau] yielded its thorns. So for thirteen years both went to school and came home from school. After this age, Jacob went to the house of study and Esau went to houses of idolatry." Rabbi Eleazar ben Rabbi Simeon said, "Parents are responsible for their children until they reach the age of thirteen. After this age, a parent must say, 'Praised is God who has now freed me from the responsibility of this boy.'"

Genesis Rabbah 63:10

Revelation

When Shall God Give the Torah?

Background: This story attempts to explain why God waited some time after the Israelites had left Egypt before giving them the Torah.

Rabbi Isaac said, "It would have made more sense for the Israelites to have received the Torah immediately after the Exodus from Egypt. But God said, 'My children have not as yet recovered. They have just been redeemed from slavery and are not in physical condition to receive the Torah.'

"This situation is comparable to the case of a young prince who had just recovered from a very serious illness when the royal tutor said to the king, 'Send the prince back to school.' But the king refused and said, 'The prince is still sick and has not fully recovered. Let him recuperate for several months and let him put on some weight, after which he can return to school.'

"Similarly God said concerning the Israelites, 'How can I give them the Torah so soon after they were freed from Egyptian slavery? It is better that they be given a chance to heal for several months and have the nourishment of manna and quail. After that, it will be time for Me to give them My Torah.'"

Various traditional sources

How the Israelites Received the Torah

Background: This story attempts to explain the reason God chose the Israelites to receive the Torah.

When God revealed the Divine Presence to Israel and was ready to give the Israelites the Torah, God appeared not only to them but also to all of the other nations. God spoke first to the children of Esau and asked them, "Will you accept My Torah?" They asked, "What is written in it?"

God answered, "You shall not murder."

"O God, how do You expect us to live with such a law? Our father, Esau, was a hunter and a murderer while Isaac, his father, promised him in a blessing that he would live only by the sword. This Torah You are offering is not for us."

Next God went to the Ammonites and the Moabites. "Will you accept My Torah?" God asked. They too wanted to know what was written in it.

God then answered, "You shall not commit adultery."

"O Sovereign Ruler," they replied, "we owe our very lives to incest. We cannot possibly live by Your Torah."

Then God went to the desert people and asked, "Will you people take My Torah?"

They replied, "Tell us first what is in Your Torah."

God replied, "'You shall not steal' is one of the laws in the Torah."

"This is not for us," replied the Ishmaelites. "Our entire lives have been connected with thievery and stealing."

The fact of the matter is that God went to all the nations of the world, asking them to receive the Torah, but each one in turn flatly refused.

Finally, the God of Israel came to the Israelites, who immediately volunteered and said, "We will obey and we will hearken" (Exodus 24:7).

Exodus Rabbah 27:9

The Baal Shem Tov Saves a Bar Mitzvah Boy

Background: This legend is one of many folktales in which the Baal Shem Tov, the founder of Hasidism, saves the life of a boy who has just reached the age of *bar mitzvah*.

In the city of Konstanty there was a man who did not have children. He visited the Baal Shem Tov on several occasions and was promised by him that one day his wife would give birth to a baby boy. Sure enough, she delivered a beautiful baby boy.

When the Baal Shem Tov heard the news, he began to cry uncontrollably. The man asked, "Why are you crying, Master?"

The Baal Shem Tov answered, "Because I see that on the day your boy becomes a *bar mitzvah*, he will be drawn into a river. Since you will probably forget about it, I'd like to give you a sign in order for you to remember."

And the Baal Shem Tov proceeded to explain to the man that on the day his son will put two stockings on one foot and search for the second one, that would be the sign. He further emphasized that when this sign came to pass, the boy must be guarded carefully and must be admonished to stay away from water.

Years passed and the matter was forgotten. On the day that the boy had his *bar mitzvah* he lost one stocking and his father noticed that he was wearing two stockings on one foot. He was immediately reminded of the warning of the Baal Shem Tov and guarded his son very carefully.

During that day the sun was very hot and everyone in the town went to the river to swim. The boy too sneaked out of his house and ran to the river. Immediately his father ran after him and brought him home. Finally, the father decided to lock up his son in a room so that there would be no possibility of his making an escape.

After the *Minchah* afternoon service, when all the townspeople were near the river, a huge creature with a head and two hands emerged from the water, slapped his hands on the water and said, "The one who is mine is not here." Then it sank into the river.

At once the boy slept soundly. With God's help he grew up and had a very long life, just as the Baal Shem Tov had promised.

Folktale

III
THE
MIDDLE
YEARS

Set me as a seal upon your heart.

Song of Songs 8:6

We recognize the social struggle of our communities over alternative lifestyles and the desire for some people to stay single. Yet for much of Jewish history marriage was assumed to be a routine part of life. It was something most people did as a matter of course. As far back as the Book of Genesis, we read, "It is not good for people to be alone. I will make a soul mate for you" (Genesis 2:18). For the people who have chosen this route, the wedding is one of the most joyous occasions in the life of two individuals—and their families. For the couple, it represents the quintessential Jewish experience, encompassing religious ritual, tradition, and creativity: a link between past and future. It is in the context of marriage that Jewish family life begins anew.

It is not surprising that there is a plethora of passages from the Bible, Midrash, and other sacred texts about love and marriage. We realize that love and marriage are not restricted to one's middle years. However, we felt that stories of love and marriage belonged in this section nonetheless. In the Middle Years section of this book, we share with you stories about the world's first wedding, matchmaking, wedding blessings, love and relationships, and stories related to wedding rituals, particularly the breaking of the glass.

In addition, this section of our collection includes several stories related to attempts to save a marriage, the pain of divorce, and an incident of divorce in later life. We know that traditionally only a man could divorce a woman, and these stories reflect this bias. We recognize, as well, that in liberal communities modernity has made the partners equally responsible in all aspects of marriage. Thus, we offer them in the context of the tradition in which they emerged.

Finally, a fairly extensive literature of stories and tales has emerged through the centuries related to Jewish conversion. In this section, you will also find stories with varied themes, including the conversion of Terach, Abraham's father, God's love of proselytes, rabbinic procedures for conversion, and how the Greek Akilas converted to Judaism. These are stories of conversion, but in the end we are all Jews, regardless of our origin.

Love

Searching for the Only One

Background: This story is a tale of mystical splendor and marital bliss that suggests that we spend our lives searching for the one person who is indeed our perfect mate, for it was to that person's soul that we were joined prior to entering this world. It is actually based on a comment from a Torah text from *parashat Lech Lecha*, "And *Adonai* spoke to Abram. After that, Lot was separated from him" (Genesis 13:14a).

Prior to birth, all of the souls in the world are mystically one. When they descend into the world, they are separated into male and female, though they are still joined in a spiritual way. They travel through life as individuals, one searching out the other, often unconscious of their task. When God feels the time is right, God mates them—God and no other. It is God alone, whose handiwork is all creation and all souls, who knows the proper mate for individual souls. Happy is the person who is upright in his works and walks in the way of truth so that her soul may find its original mate. Then indeed they both become perfect, and through their perfection the whole world is blessed.

Based on *Zohar* I, 85b

Switched at Birth

Background: As parents, we often compare our children with those of our neighbors. In this story of Rabbi Judah Loew of Prague (and his golem), we learn what can happen when we try to manipulate the events regarding God's creation of children.

In the days when Rabbi Loew was chief judge of the Jewish community of Prague, there lived two very successful men who were partners in business. They purchased a big, new home and lived there together. Only in one area were they different. Both were married and had children. The children of one of the men were robust and healthy, but the children of the second man were sickly and often did not survive. This second man's spouse was very jealous of her neighbor and the happiness she enjoyed from her children. She hid her feelings, but the midwife who cared for them both knew the true pain she endured each time she gave birth.

On one occasion, both women gave birth to children at the same time. Both babies were boys. Noticing that the son of one mother seemed healthier than the son of the second, the midwife decided to exchange the children. She carried out this plan in silence, while all of the family members were sound asleep.

Each woman nursed the child she imagined to be her son. The two boys grew up, never realizing that their parents were really not their own. The midwife told no one of her deed and carried her secret to the grave.

Eventually the boys grew to an age when they wished to marry. The father of the healthy children decided that his youngest son (really his neighbor's son) should wed the daughter of his closest friend and partner. The *tena'im* agreement (deed of betrothal) was written and the wedding day soon arrived. Rabbi Loew was expected to officiate at the wedding ceremony, but a strange thing happened. At the very moment when the rabbi was prepared to recite the benediction, the cup that held the wine suddenly shattered in his hand. Another glass was handed to him, but it too broke into pieces.

The rabbi turned pale—and the guests became very frightened. The event could only be determined as an omen that foretold no good. The *golem* was sent for more wine; guests noticed him exchanging glances with someone who did not appear to be there. When the *golem* reached the door to the cellar, he suddenly stood still, then hurried into Rabbi Loew's study. Here he scribbled a few words on a slip of paper and then handed the paper to Rabbi Loew. When the rabbi saw what was written, he was terribly frightened. On the paper was written, "Bride and groom are brother and sister."

The rabbi glanced at the *golem* and then at the assembled guests, telling them the wedding could not take place that day. He asked the parents to distribute all the food that had been prepared to the poor. He quickly left and, in front of the synagogue, beheld the spirit that had told the *golem* of the relationship between bride and groom.

Rabbi Loew decided to investigate the matter and unravel the mystery. Following daily services the next morning, he asked the congregation to remain in the synagogue a bit. Earlier the rabbi had instructed his staff to erect a partition made from wood in a corner of the room. Then he sat down with two assistant judges at a table. The *shammas* was sent to bring the bridal couple and their parents. When they all appeared, Rabbi Loew told the *golem* to go the cemetery to fetch the spirit of the deceased midwife. He handed the *golem* his stick, which he was to use to knock upon the midwife's grave and rouse her from her eternal sleep. Everyone was afraid, but Rabbi Loew eased their fears.

Everyone waited in an atmosphere of tense silence when the *golem* returned and handed the stick back to Rabbi Loew, first pointing to the partition as if to indicate that the dead women's spirit was lingering behind it. The small group became even more fearful. They closed their eyes and were stone-faced while the rabbi called out to the spirit, "We, the earthly court of justice, command you to speak and tell the truth regarding the bridal couple and answer the question of how they are brother and sister."

The soul of the midwife began to speak and to tell all of what had happened on the night that the two boys were born. While the members of the community—who were listening outside—could only hear the voice of the speaker but could distinguish no words, the judges and the members of the family heard all. The dead woman confessed that in the twelve years she had spent in the grave, she had found no rest. It was only because of Rabbi Loew that she now would finally be able to rest. She began to weep and the community joined her, sobbing loudly.

Rabbi Loew conferred with his assistants in order to decide what should be done. The rabbis determined that the midwife should ask forgiveness of the couple—which, filled with remorse, she quickly did. She was then allowed to depart peacefully. Since the brother and sister were brought up as friends—and not as siblings—they were told to marry, an instruction they happily were prepared to follow.

Based on *Niflaot Maharal*

King Solomon's Daughter

Background: Parents often want to participate in the selection of the life partners of their children. Even when they try to prevent relationships from developing—especially when they misjudge their child's own instincts—their efforts will be foiled. This story provides us with evidence for such a claim.

It is said that King Solomon's daughter was more beautiful than all of the women in the land of Israel. By watching the stars, he was able to determine whom she should wed. To his dismay, he discovered that the man to whom she should be wed was the poorest person in all of ancient Israel. So what did he do? He built a tower out in the sea with walls around the tower on all sides. He then placed his daughter in the tower and surrounded her with seventy eunuchs from the elders of Israel. He built the tower with no entrances and proclaimed aloud, "Now let me see Your acts."

Eventually, the daughter's intended partner set out on a journey. Since he was barefoot, starving, and thirsty, he had nothing on which to bed for the night. From afar, he saw the carcass of a large animal and crawled between its ribs in order to stay warm for the night. Just when he fell asleep, along came a large bird that took the carcass in its teeth, carrying the man along with it, and carried his burden to Solomon's daughter's tower. There the bird consumed the flesh that remained on the animal's carcass and then flew away, leaving the man on the tower.

When the sun rose the next morning, the young woman took a walk and saw the man sleeping on her roof.

Somewhat surprised, she queried, "Who are you and how did you get here?" Came the response, "I am a Jew from the city of Akko. A bird brought me here." Concerned about his well-being, she brought him into her chamber, washed and fed him, and found that beneath the dirt was the most handsome man in all of Israel.

The two young people fell in love, their souls linked together. Since the young man was also a scribe, he decided to prepare a wedding document for the two. Using his own blood as ink, and with her consent, he proclaimed, "With *Adonai* this day, let the angels Michael and Gabriel serve as witnesses." That night they made love.

Some weeks later, the elders who had been guarding Solomon's daughter noticed that she appeared to be pregnant. "It is true," she told them, "but it is none of your business." The elders became frightened, fearful of what Solomon might do to them when he learned that his daughter had become pregnant under their protection. Nevertheless, they sent word to Solomon that he should come to the tower. When he arrived, they told him about the state of things, begging him for mercy. Solomon summoned his daughter, who told her father, "The Holy Blessed One brought me a handsome young man with whom I have been wed." So Solomon called forth the young man and questioned him about his family. Solomon soon realized that this was the man he had recognized in the stars. So Solomon rejoiced, "Praised is the Ever Present, who gives a person what is due." That is the message of the verse "God sets the single ones to dwell in homes" (Psalm 68:7).

Based on Tanchuma

Still Single

Background: Often when children grow older and they have not married, parents worry. They want their children to be happy and they perceive this as only being possible through marriage. Some people go to drastic measures when trying to "help the situation," as you will see as this story unfolds.

When Rabbi Judah Halevi's daughter had grown into maturity, her mother frequently asked her father when he would help find a suitable spouse for their daughter. Finally, Judah Halevi lost patience and said, "I swear that the first man to enter my home shall become my son-in-law."

Minutes after he made this declaration, an itinerant beggar entered the poet's home. He appeared ragged, uncouth, and ignorant. Halevi's wife was frightened at the prospect of having such a man become the husband of her daughter but knew that such an oath must be upheld. So the beggar was taken into their home, cleaned up, and given food and clothing. Next, Halevi sought to teach him the fundamentals of the Hebrew language.

At the time, the poet had been working on a composition about Purim and was unable to come up with a suitable last stanza. While Halevi was out for a walk in the neighborhood, the stranger went into Halevi's study and composed the missing few lines with language that was striking in its beauty and depth of meaning.

When Halevi returned from his walk, ready to continue his work, he was mystified. "Who wrote these words? Only an angel—or perhaps Abraham ibn Ezra—could construct such beautiful language."

"Ibn Ezra indeed wrote it," said the indigent stranger, disclosing that he was none other than the poet philosopher Halevi himself admired.

Source unknown

An All-Consuming Love

Background: This talmudic story emphasizes the strong rabbinic view regarding sexual chastity between partners before marriage.

A man once developed a great passion for a certain woman, and his heart became consumed by his burning desire for her. When the doctors were consulted, they said, "His only cure will be if she submits to his desire."

When the sages heard this advice, they said, "Let him die rather than have him yield."

The doctors then said, "Let her at least stand naked before him."

The sages replied, "It would be better if he died."

Then the doctors said, "Then let her speak with him from behind a curtain."

But the sages still maintained that it would be better if he were to die rather than even have her speak with him from behind a curtain.

Rabbi Isaac concluded that nothing—not even marriage—would satisfy this man's passion. He said, "Since the time of the destruction of the Temple, sexual pleasure has been removed from those who practice it lawfully and given to sinners, as it is written, 'Stolen waters are sweet, and bread eaten in secret is pleasant' [Proverbs 9:17]."

Babylonian Talmud, *Sanhedrin* 75a

Marriage

Marriage Advice from the Maggid of Mezritch

Background: For centuries Jewish people used the services of professional matchmakers in order to match a man with a woman for the purpose of marriage. This is a story about one such matchmaker.

A young student spent the Holy Days with the Maggid of Mezritch. When he was about to leave, he complained to his teacher, "Because I am so very poor, no matchmaker comes to me with a suitable bride. I am getting older and more worried each day."

The Maggid told him to go in peace and accept the first marriage proposal that was made to him.

The young student was pleased with this advice and went on his way. That night, he stopped at a village inn for a night's sleep. There he met a group of carefree young people who had had too much to drink and were looking for a good time at someone else's expense.

"Where are you from?" asked one of the youths to the young student.

"I have come from a holiday visit to my teacher," he answered. "And I have been told to accept the first marriage proposal that should come my way."

"I have the perfect match," answered one young man, thinking that this would be a terrific hoax. "I have a young sister who was just divorced. She possesses a dowry of one hundred rubles, and if you wish, we will immediately arrange for your engagement."

Of course, all of this was false. The jokester had no

sister and instead invited the innkeeper's daughter to play along in the ruse. The naive young student agreed and decided at that moment to write out his own marriage contract and perform his own wedding.

All was made ready—the *chuppah*, the glasses of wine, and the ring. The young student placed the ring on his bride's right index finger, and all the witnesses cried out, "*Mazel tov.*"

Then something seemed to be wrong. The merry-makers started to push the young man around and the party grew rougher and tougher. Frightened by this turn of events, the young student decided to seek refuge in a nearby house.

The next morning he returned to the inn to reclaim his belongings. As he was standing in front of the house, a carriage arrived and he heard some of the servants say, "The boss is back."

Gathering up his strength, he approached the boss and said, "Good morning, father-in-law."

"Who is this?" demanded the boss. His daughter, who was standing nearby, told her father about the joke that had been played. However, the father investigated the situation and soon concluded that a valid marriage ceremony had indeed been performed. In anger, he struck the young man in the face, realizing what had transpired.

Soon he realized that he would need the young man's cooperation in order to have the marriage dissolved. "I will give you twenty rubles if you agree to a divorce," he said.

"This was no joke to me," blurted the young man. "I am legally married and if you are not in agreement, let us both go to the rabbi and let him make the decision."

The rabbi decided to have a meeting with the young man, after which he returned to the father. "I spoke to the young man about a divorce," he said to the father. "He has agreed to release your daughter, provided that you give him one thousand rubles! I also will arrange a match for your daughter with a fine young man who is worth one thousand rubles."

The father agreed. When the rabbi heard this he said, "I want you to know that this young man comes from a very important family. He is very learned, although he is very poor. Now that he has one thousand rubles, however, his financial problem is solved as well. I see no better match for your daughter than this same young man. The match was made in heaven. Go home and take this young man home with you, for he will make your daughter an excellent husband."

The innkeeper agreed, and he and his new son-in-law went home in a happy frame of mind. And the match turned out to be a true success!

Chasidic story

The Right Yichus

Background: In Eastern Europe during the 1800s, most people lived in small villages called shtetls or *shtetlach*. The houses were built close to one another and the people were close too. They knew one another's family stories and secrets, some of which determined the family's *yichus* (credentials). *Yichus* was achieved through learning, earning, and being descended from a famous rabbi. Health was important too. A sickly ancestor was a black mark against the family, and so was a red-haired ancestor or even a left-handed one. While we may debate the logic of some of these beliefs, that's just the way it was!

In a small village in Eastern Europe lived a matchmaker, also called a *shadchan*, whose name was Nachman the Shadchan. He kept books in which he recorded who was born a girl, who was born a boy, and when each was born. Also, he recorded which families were learned and which were ignorant; which were rich and which were poor; which were healthy and which were sickly. That's just the way it was!

A *shadchan* ensured that marriage matches were made strictly according to the rules: rich married rich, and poor married poor. Learned married learned, and ignorant married ignorant. For his services, the *shadchan* received a flat fee and a percentage of the dowry. To marry without the services of a *shadchan* was a disgrace. In those days, whoever dared to be different was shamed in the village and became a target of gossip. That's just the way it was!

One day, after consulting his records, Nachman decided it was time to visit Shmuel ben David and his wife,

Sorah Leah, regarding their son Berel. He announced, "I have come to see you about your oldest son, Berel. He is almost a man and it is time to find him a wife. Don't you agree?" "If you really think so," replied Shmuel, "but what Berel likes best is to learn. A student spends his days and nights learning and is only interested in books. I don't know if he is ready for marriage."

Sorah Leah interrupted, "Of course Berel needs a wife! He needs a wife with a good dowry and from a learned family to match his own talents. It should be a family rich enough to support him in his studies. Who knows? With the right wife, someday Berel may become a *talmid chacham* [a wise student]. Regarding our family's *yichus*," she continued, "why, my great grandfather was close to the Bobover Rebbe, and Shmuel is a direct descendant of a scribe [Nachman remembered that he had heard someone say "a servant"] in the court of David, king of Israel."

"I shall start to work on a bride for Berel right away," agreed Nachman, "and you should start to save for a dowry for your daughter, Devorah-Liba. Soon she will be fifteen. Did you see the ox cart driver's son eyeing her? With a good dowry, we can get better for her."

Parents of the bride had to give a dowry—money and other gifts—to start the young couple off in marriage. Often, they had to pay all of the pair's expenses for several years. What did the bridegroom's family give? They gave their son. That's just the way it was!

For an entire year, Nachman presented girls of marriageable age from suitable families to Berel. The girls liked Berel. With his unruly brown hair that fell over his forehead and heavy-lidded eyes that kept stealing glances at the pages of his book even as they visited, he was a romantic figure. But Berel, if he noticed each girl at all, would shrug his shoulders and say, "Too tall" or "Too short," "Too fat" or "Too thin." At other times, the girl was "too bold" or "too timid." To tell you the truth, Berel was not really interested. That's just the way it was!

The day arrived when the supply of eligible girls in their village and in the neighboring villages was used up. Nachman began to consult other matchmakers from villages that were one whole day's, even two days' journey away, which meant that he would have to split his fee with them. He did not like it, but what could he do? That's just the way it was!

One day, Nachman burst into Shmuel's makeshift office in the marketplace with what he considered an offer Berel could not refuse. "Shmuel," Nachman called. "What an opportunity! What an opportunity! Three days' journey away, in a town called Mooshlik, lives a rich merchant and his family. This merchant has only one daughter, Ruchel, upon whom he and his wife dote, and the Mooshlik *shadchan* says that when the merchant heard that Berel is a *lerner* [student of Torah], he was very impressed. Shmuel, the merchant wants to meet Berel. If the merchant approves, then Berel can meet his daughter, Ruchel."

Shmuel's bearded face saddened. "So far away. . . ."

"Shmuel," continued Nachman, already counting his fee, "the merchant said if everything works out, he is promising not only to support Berel and Ruchel and to provide them with a home and a gift of money but also, listen Shmuel, he has offered to settle some money on Berel's parents as well." That's not usually the way it was; it was better!

Shmuel went home to tell his wife, Sorah Leah. "Can you imagine," she said, hurriedly wiping the flour off her hands, "Berel could spend his life in study. Perhaps he could become a great scholar of Talmud. And we, we would have a nest egg to start our daughter Devorah-Liba's dowry. Oy, it is a match made in heaven," she crooned. "And what if Berel doesn't like her?" Shmuel asked.

"Like, *shmike*," replied Sorah Leah, "he'll marry her and that's that." That's just the way it was!

Nachman, Shmuel, and Berel set out the following morning. At midnight on their third day of travel, they reached Mooshlik. Mooshlik was more a town than a village, with a great square cobbled in stone at its center. In a prominent place at the edge of the square stood the merchant's house. By the moonlight, they could see how impressive it was. It was the largest house on the square. There was nothing like it in their village or in all the villages around.

The shop, announced by a broad gold sign with red lettering above its door, was on the street level; the family's living quarters were above. At the side of the house a lantern was left burning. This was where they were to enter. A servant greeted them and showed them to their lodgings.

The same servant awakened them the next morning. "Breakfast is being served and my master awaits your company," he said. Berel, as usual, was hunched over, reading, hair falling over his forehead, and had to be poked to follow them into the dining room. That's just the way it was!

They found the family seated at a long wooden table. Their host, a stout, handsome man with broad shoulders, ruddy face, brown eyes, and rich brown hair, sat at the head of the table. To his right sat his wife, a fair-skinned woman with pale blue eyes that were in startling contrast to her jet-black *sheitel*, a wig worn by some pious Jewish women. She kept patting the top of it nervously, pushing it down lower on her forehead.

The talk covered many topics, from the policies of the czar, the price of wheat and wood, to the interpretations of stories told by a wonder rebbe. Throughout breakfast, the girl, Ruchel, did not appear. Nachman figured that the merchant wanted to be sure of them before he introduced her to Berel. When breakfast was over, the wife rose. Giving her hair a final tug, she announced, "We will have tea and little cakes in the parlor."

Nachman and Shmuel were amazed—a parlor in addition to a dining room. This family was wealthy indeed. To tell the truth, neither Nachman nor Shmuel were used to such grand houses or grand ways. It made Shmuel nervous, but Nachman—he was gearing up to negotiate the marriage contract. God willing, there would be an agreement within an hour and he, Nachman, would be on his way home with his pocket heavier by a goodly sum.

Shmuel shivered. Rich, *shmich*, he began to be sorry they had come. What business did his son have to marry into such a rich family? He would have gotten up to leave, except he was afraid of what his wife, Sorah Leah, would say to him. She would be furious if he let this opportunity get away. The three followed their hosts and settled themselves.

The servant set a large tray table with china cups and saucers, a cream pitcher, sugar bowl, and a pot of tea fresh from the samovar, in front of the wife. She leaned forward and began to pour. Then the servant returned, leading a large black dog by a strong leather strap, and wound the handle of the strap around the merchant's chair. The dog settled himself comfortably at the merchant's feet. The sight of the dog increased their uneasiness. Everything was different about Mooshlik, but most of all, this merchant and his family. Jews didn't have dogs. Jews had cats to chase mice. Dogs were the pets of peasants who used them to torment Jews. Shmuel glanced over at Nachman, whose face showed no expression.

At last, Nachman spoke. "Everything looks delicious, dear madame, but when will we have the pleasure of meeting your lovely daughter?" "As a matter of fact," said the wife, "I am about to call her now." She took a silver bell from the table and gently waved it back and forth. It made a light tinkling sound.

Immediately, in walked a tall, broad-shouldered girl, her hair covered modestly by a fine white linen scarf. The girl smiled at them as she entered. "Here are the cakes," she said quietly, "and here am I, Ruchel." Berel glanced at her without much interest. Then all of a sudden, Ruchel's hand reached to the scarf and ripped it from her head. A cascade of fiery red hair spilled out. Berel was fascinated. "I will not get married under false pretenses," the girl said. She looked directly at Berel. "If you want me, take me as I am, red hair and all; otherwise, I do not want you!" Berel was enchanted. His usually bland face creased into a smile.

Nachman saw his large commission flying out the window. He wondered if he would have to pay the *shadchan* of Mooshlik for his time and trouble. Whatever it cost him, he would pay. One thing he knew for sure. This match would never take place. Nachman the *shadchan* would not tarnish his reputation by making a match with a red-haired bride. For all they knew, she might even be left-handed too. That was not at all the way it was supposed to be.

Shmuel was totally confused. What did it all mean? Berel looked happy and alert for the first time in his life, but Nachman was glowering. What would Sorah Leah want him to do? He wished she were here. Nachman began to rise to his feet. So did the dog. Nachman sat down. The dog remained standing.

"Shmuel," hissed Nachman, "get up. We've got to get Berel out of here." Shmuel started to rise hesitantly. The dog pulled back his lips, showing his teeth, and growled deep in his throat. Shmuel sat down. The merchant sounded amused, but he wasn't smiling. "Aren't you used to dogs?" he asked mildly.

This time Nachman motioned to Shmuel for each to grab an arm of the enchanted Berel—who continued to sit between them—and drag him out of the room. They started to do so. The dog's ears flattened on his head. His growl grew more menacing and the hairs on his neck stood bolt upright.

They let go of Berel's arms and all sat down. "So," said the merchant, "are we agreed?" "I am agreed," Berel said eagerly. Ruchel smiled broadly at him and replaced her scarf. "I guess that I am agreed, also," said Shmuel, eyeing the dog at his left hip and his animated son at his right. "Then there is nothing further for me to say," said Nachman, and the *tena'im* (betrothal documents) were signed.

And that is how Nachman the *shadchan* lost his reputation as the finest *shadchan* in Eastern Europe and how in each generation, a red-haired baby is born into our family.

Traditional tale retold by Marcia Posner

The Marriage Question

Background: There are many stories in Jewish tradition that deal with the theme of how rabbis attempt to find suitable mates for their daughters. In this story, the criterion for a suitable mate is based on Torah scholarship.

Rabbi Eizel Charif, the Rabbi of Slonim, had a daughter whom he wanted to see married. He decided to travel to Volozhin to seek out a suitable husband for his daughter.

Arriving in Volozhin, he got the word out to all prospective suitors that the one who showed the most outstanding Torah scholarship would be the one chosen for his daughter.

Rabbi Eizel posed a question to the potential suitors, and one by one each tried to answer it. However, Rabbi Eizel rejected every single answer. Not one student could find a solution to the question.

Finally, it came time for the rabbi to go home. The community of Volozhin was embarrassed that he would be leaving without a match for his daughter. Suddenly, as the community members were saying their good-byes, one young yeshivah student came forward and said, "Match or no marriage match, tell us please, Rabbi, what is the answer to the question?"

Rabbi Eizel paused in amazement and then replied, "You, young man, are the one I want for my daughter. Any person who is interested in learning Torah for its own sake, and not for any other reason, is the one I want for my daughter!"

Adapted from the parables of Rabbi Sholom Schwadron, the Maggid of Jerusalem

A Match Made in Heaven

Background: This story is a reminder that God is the ultimate Matchmaker and that even God has to work diligently in order to make a successful match of husband and wife.

Once, a Roman matron asked Rabbi Yose bar Halafta, "How long did it take God to create the world?"

He said to her, "Six days."

"And from then until now, what has God been doing?" she inquired.

"God has been occupied in making marriages," came Rabbi Yose's response.

"And is that God's occupation?" the woman asked. "Even I can do that. I have many male and female slaves, and in one short hour I can marry all of them off."

"Although it may appear easy in your eyes," the rabbi said, "every marriage is as difficult for the Sovereign of Sovereigns as the dividing of the Red Sea." Then Rabbi Yose left her and went on his way.

What did the woman do? She took one thousand male slaves and one thousand female slaves, put them in two rows, and said, "This one should wed that one, and this one should wed that one." In one night, she married them all! The next day they came to her—one with a wounded head, one with a bruised eye, another with a broken toe.

"What is the matter with all of you?" she asked.

Each one answered, "I do not want the one you selected for me."

Immediately, the woman sent for Rabbi Yose bar Halafta and said to him, "Rabbi, your Torah is true and beautiful."

"Indeed, a suitable match may seem easy to make, but God considers it as difficult a task as dividing the Red Sea," Rabbi Yose acknowledged.

Genesis Rabbah 68:4

The First Wedding

Background: This midrashic story is our reminder that the very first marriage was between Adam and Eve, and of God's important role in a Jewish marriage.

The wedding of the first couple was celebrated with great festivities. Before presenting Eve to Adam, God dressed her like a bride. Appealing to the angels, God said, "Let us perform services of friendship for Adam and his helpmate, for the world itself rests upon friendly services."

The angels of God surrounded the marriage canopy and God pronounced the wedding blessings. The angels danced while playing musical instruments.

Adam called his wife *Ishah*, and he called himself *Ish*, abandoning the name Adam, which he had originally been given. He did this because God included God's own Name in the name of man and woman—*yod* in *Ish* and *heh* in *Ishah*—to indicate that as long as man and woman would walk in God's ways that God's Name would shield them from any harm.

But if man and woman would ever go astray and leave God's ways, then God would withdraw the Divine Name from them, and instead of *Ish* and *Ishah* there would remain *esh*, fire, which would consume the both of them.

Pirke de Rabbi Eliezer 12:1

Hillel's Wife Helps the Poor

Background: In this talmudic story, Hillel's wife prepares the festive wedding meal for a poor couple.

Rabbi Hillel was a poor man. His wife would prepare all of their meals by herself. Once, an important guest came to visit Hillel. Wanting to treat him properly, Hillel turned to his wife and said, "Please prepare a tasty meal for our guest."

Hillel's wife rushed to the kitchen and prepared a delectable meal, including homemade bread. When she was about to bring the food out to the table, a knock was heard at the door. Opening the door, she saw a young man who looked very sad and forlorn.

"May I help you?" she asked the young man.

The man responded, "It is the day of my wedding today, but we are a poor couple, and we have no means to prepare our wedding meal. I feel so ashamed."

Hillel's wife immediately took all of the food that she had prepared for her houseguest and gave it to the young man. The poor man gratefully accepted the gift of food and hastened to his wedding, where a festive meal was enjoyed by all.

What did Hillel's wife do now? She started all of her preparations anew, baking bread and preparing the meal all over again.

All of this time Hillel and his guest were studying Torah. The hour was getting late, and Hillel and his guest were getting hungry. Although he was surprised that his wife had not brought them the meal, he remained silent.

At long last his wife came in with the sumptuous meal.

"Why didn't you serve us right away?" Hillel asked.

His wife told him the entire story of how she gave the prepared meal to a poor groom.

Hearing this, Hillel was very pleased and said, "My dear, you did this for the sake of heaven! God will be very pleased with your deeds of kindness!"

Babylonian Talmud, *Derech Eretz*, chapter 6

Wedding Blessing

Background: This talmudic story presents us with a beautiful wedding blessing. It has become well known because it is often used by contemporary rabbis in their charge to a bride and groom during their wedding.

A storyteller once attended the wedding of two friends. At a certain point in the ceremony, while they were still under the *chuppah*, the couple turned to the storyteller and asked, "Would you give us your blessing?"

"Yes," replied the storyteller, "but a storyteller gives a blessing by telling a story." And this was her story.

Once, a man was making a journey across a desert. Soon he became hungry and thirsty, as you can imagine, and weary too. He looked around to see if there was any place where he could stop and rest. There before him was a tree with wide branches and leaves and beautiful fruit. Beneath the tree was a flowing stream. The man ate of the fruit and drank of the water. Then he sat under the branches to rest in their shade, and soon he felt refreshed and strong.

When he was ready to continue his journey, the man said to the tree, "O Tree, *O Elan*, How shall I bless you? *Bameh avarechecha?*

"Shall I say, 'May your fruit be sweet?' Your fruit is already sweet. 'May your shade be pleasant?' Your shade is cool and pleasant already. 'May you have a stream of flowing water beneath you?' But you already have a flowing stream that refreshes and feeds both you and traveler! *O Elan*, O Tree, How shall I bless you? May it be God's will that all the offshoots taken from you be like you."

"And so, my dear friends, bride and groom, I too ask, With what shall I bless you?" asked the storyteller. "You already have the fruit of friendship made sweeter by helping others and giving others a sense of comfort. You have beautiful branches that reach out to one another to offer protection with your feelings, thoughts—and silence. You also have flowing water, your sense of spirituality and wisdom.

"Then how shall I bless you?

"May it be God's will that all the works you create together and the children you have and love together will all be like you. May it be God's will."

"The Wedding Blessing," from *Jewish Stories One Generation Tells Another*, retold by Peninnah Schram.

Breaking the Glass

Background: While there are many customs around the world regarding the bridal canopy, the most widely practiced is certainly the breaking of the glass, which probably dates back to the fifth century and is explained in the Talmud.

Rab Ashi had invited some of his colleagues to a banquet to celebrate the wedding of his son. Great joy was felt until Rab Ashi, finding the merriment a bit exhausting and somewhat excessive, sought to moderate it. So he broke an expensive crystal goblet—to the amazement of his guests—in the middle of the hall. The general joy immediately abated and silence fell upon the celebration. That was exactly what the pious rabbi had intended. He wanted to remind everyone of the fragility of humankind and our mortal existence. In the midst of great joy, we should be reminded that we are all but passing shadows.

Based on Babylonian Talmud, *Berachot* 30a

Honoring the Bride and Groom

Background: This story is a reminder of the responsibility to honor the bride at her wedding by attending to her.

If two scholars sit and study the Torah and a bridal procession passes before them, if there are a sufficient number of people in the wedding procession, then they should not neglect their study. However, if there is an inadequate number of people, then let them get up and cheer and hail the bride.

Once, as Rabbi Judah bar Ilai sat teaching his students, a bride passed by. He took myrtle twigs in his hand and cheered her until the bride passed out of his sight.

Another time, as Rabbi Judah bar Ilai sat teaching his students, a bride passed by. "What was that?" he asked them.

They replied, "A bride passing by."

"My sons," he said to them, "get up and attend to the bride. For thus we find concerning the Holy One that God attended to a bride, as it is written, 'And God built the rib' [Genesis 2:22]. If God attended to the bride, how much more so should we!"

And if you should ask, "When do we find that God attended to a bride?" it is written, "And God built the rib." Now in the sea towns they call braiding hair *binyata* (building). In this way we truly learn that God braided Eve's hair and outfitted her as a bride and brought her to Adam.

Avot de Rabbi Natan, chapter 4

Wedding Behavior

Background: During the wedding of the sons of two *amora'im*, three unusual events occurred. Such events were considered rather puzzling. This tale attempts to explain the unusual behavior and teach about redemption at the same time.

It seems that at the feast following the wedding of Mar bar Ravina's son, the sages were filled with joy. Then one of the guests looked at their host and said to the man seated next to him, "Why does he seem so upset?"

"Look what he is about to do!" came the reply.

The entire assembly turned their attention to Mar bar Ravina. In his hand, he held a very expensive crystal glass. He took the glass, raised it high, and then flung it to the ground. As a result, of course, it shattered into thousands of little pieces.

Everyone was dumbstruck. No one dared say a word. Then suddenly, one person whispered to the person sitting next to him, "The goblet was worth a fortune." He had spoken quietly, but amidst the silence in the banquet hall, every word could easily be heard. From the end of the table, another person replied, "Yes, four hundred *zuz* [a lot of money]."

What had prompted Mar to do what seemed to be a rather peculiar thing? Why had he chosen to stop the celebration of his son's wedding with what appeared to be such a foolish act? In a few brief seconds, he had changed joy into bewilderment. After a few very long minutes, people tried to return to their conversations and their general partying. One person encouraged another, "Sing something for us, Rabbi Hamnuna. You know so well how to gladden the heart of a [bride and] groom." Hamnuna began singing, but the words were those of despair: "Alas, we must all die. Alas, we must all die."

"But what chorus shall we sing to such a song?" they asked.

"Where is the Torah and where are the mitzvot that will protect us from the judgment of Gehinnom?" came his answer.

When Rabbi Ashi's son was married, he acted similarly to Mar bar Ravina. He took a priceless silver goblet and hurled it against the wall. Following the crash came silence; the rejoicing abruptly came to an end.

Why had both men acted so strangely in the midst of their children's wedding feasts? Should they not have "gladdened the heart of the bride and groom," as the Talmud instructs us?

The answer to the riddle comes in the words of Rabbi Yochanan, who taught in the name of Rabbi Shimon bar Yochai: "A person is forbidden to enjoy a full measure of laughter in this world, as it says, 'Then shall our mouths be filled with laughter.' And when will that time occur? When 'the nations say, God has done great wonders with them.' When the Messiah comes and brings ultimate redemption to the Jewish people all over the world. Only then will we be able to laugh as much as we want to."

When Mar bar Ravina, Rabbi Ashi, and Rabbi Hamnuna saw their friends' joy reaching growing levels of ecstasy, they were afraid they might reach beyond the permitted level of joy. They sought to bring them down to earth and remind them that the time of ultimate joy and ultimate redemption had not yet come.

Based on Babylonian Talmud, *Berachot* 30b

The Wedding Bite

Background: This is a story about Rabbi Akiba's reaction to astrology, a school of thought that he purportedly did not accept as valid.

Rabbi Akiba taught that there is no *mazal* (astrology and fate). Rabbi Akiba had a daughter. The astrologers told Akiba that she would die on her wedding day as a result of a snakebite. Akiba was very worried. On the day of her wedding, Akiba's daughter took off her brooch and stuck it in the fence. It so happened that the point of the brooch penetrated the eye of a snake. On the following morning, she removed the brooch and a snake was hanging from it. Her father was bewildered [and assumed that she had been rewarded for a good deed]. "What did you do?" he asked. She said, "Last evening, a poor person came to the door. Everyone was busy at the wedding banquet and paid him no attention. I took my plate to the poor man and gave it to him." Akiba said to his daughter, "You performed a *mitzvah*," and he quoted the text "Charity delivers from death" (Proverbs 10:2), not only from an unnatural death, but from death in general.

Babylonian Talmud, *Shabbat* 156b

The Bride's Prayer

Background: This talmudic story provides us with a glimpse of a legendary wedding in ancient times.

Once there lived a very pious man who had no children. He prayed and prayed for a son, and vowed that if one was born, he would invite every poor person to his wedding feast. Eventually a son was born to him, and he called him Mattaniah, meaning a gift from God. The boy grew up and his wedding day approached. The father invited all students of the Torah and the poor to the reception, which filled up six rooms!

God wanted to test the bridegroom, so God sent the Angel of Death disguised in dirty clothes to beg for a place at the wedding. The bridegroom refused based on the fact that all had already been invited and that the man's clothing was soiled.

In the night the Angel of Death revealed himself, declaring that he was about to take away the bridegroom's soul since he had failed the test. Hearing this, the bride prayed to God, "Sovereign of the Universe, You have said in Your Torah that when a man takes a wife, he shall bring her cheer for one full year and not leave her. May it be Your will, O God, that my husband will live so that I can teach him to practice loving-kindness without discrimination."

Her prayer was heard on high, and the Angel of Death was commanded to leave. What was the nature of this young woman? Her mother was accustomed to draw cool water from a spring for school-age children. When she became old, her daughter said, "You don't have to abandon your good deeds. I shall give you the strength of my arm and carry most of the weight so that you can continue to perform the *mitzvah*."

It was this consideration for her mother that made her so very deserving in the eyes of God.

Midrash Asseret Hadibrot

The Marriage of Akiba and Rachel

Background: This story relates the concern of a father who finds that his daughter has fallen in love with a poor and illiterate man.

Before Rabbi Akiba became a famous scholar, he worked as a shepherd in Jerusalem for Kalba Sabua, a wealthy farmer. Kalba Sabua had a very beautiful daughter named Rachel, who became attracted to Akiba because of his modesty. One day she said to him, "If I marry you, will you go and study Torah?"

Although he knew that his future studies would take him far away from Rachel, he married her in secret and then went away to study.

When Kalba Sabua, Rachel's father, found out about their marriage, he became livid. How could she marry such an illiterate and poor man?

Kalba removed his daughter from his house and promised never to give her any of his money.

At age forty, Akiba set out to study Torah. One day, stopping at a waterfall, he saw the steady dripping of water wearing away a solid rock. He then realized that the water of Torah would be able to wear away his ignorance. He studied Torah for twelve years, returning home with twelve thousand students.

Rachel was overjoyed to see him, but when an elderly woman mocked her and compared her to a widow, Rachel said she would be pleased if her husband Akiba studied Torah for an additional twelve years. Hearing this, Akiba went away to a different school and returned home with an additional twelve thousand students.

Upon his arrival home this time, his wife came out to greet him.

Akiba's students noticed how poorly dressed Rachel was and began to push her away from their teacher—not realizing that this woman was Akiba's wife. But Akiba said, "Do not push her away. It is she who is truly responsible for my Torah knowledge." It was then that he told his students all about his secret marriage.

When Kalba heard that a famous rabbi had arrived in the city, he decided to ask the wise man to absolve him of his vow, for he loved his daughter very much and regretted what he had said to her.

Kalba came to Rabbi Akiba and told the rabbi of his regret for his hasty actions, explaining his anger at his daughter's betrothal to a simple shepherd boy. Rabbi Akiba then said to him, "If this shepherd boy had been a learned man, would you still have made your vow?"

Kalba responded, "If this shepherd boy knew even a single chapter of Torah, I would not have made the vow."

Rabbi Akiba then confessed, "You don't recognize me, but I am the shepherd who married your daughter. She was the one who allowed me to go far away from her and study."

Hearing this, Kalba sank to his knees and offered the rabbi half of his wealth in thanksgiving.

Adapted from Babylonian Talmud, *Ketubot* 62b–63a; *Nedarim* 50a

Two Sisters

Background: This tale is about two sisters. While one was wealthy and the other was poor, each was envious of the other. It seems that we are seldom content with our lot; nor do we appreciate the value of real wealth..

Once there were two sisters who married and lived in towns distant from each other. As often happens with siblings, one sister found herself quite wealthy, while the other was very poor. Because of the great distance that separated them, they could see each other only once every several years. When that happened, each one would tell the other everything that had happened since the previous encounter.

Once when the poor sister went to visit the wealthy one, she was stunned at her wealthy sister's appearance. "Why do you look so run down?" she inquired. "You are prosperous, with nothing to worry about. You always have everything you want. So why do you look so terrible?"

The wealthy sister opened her heart to her poor sister and told the bitter story of her life, the one she had hidden for so many years. The poor sister was aghast. She could hardly believe what she was being told. But her wealthy sister assured her that the entire story was true, that she had never found happiness in her life. "What is the use of all this money" she wept, "if it does not help me find happiness? I can tell only you, my sister, the truth. My wealthy husband treats me horribly. He makes my life miserable. He treats me with no respect, humiliating me at every opportunity. Sometimes I don't even know how I go on living this way. You ask me why I look so terrible. It is from living this lie. You may have a hard life, always worried about household expenses. Yet you look calm and serene. It is you who are really wealthy."

"Well, you are right, my dear sister," said the other. "It is all the result of my spouse. We work hard but we work together. He has a wonderful disposition, far better than mine. It is he who makes my life so peaceful—even with all of our financial worries."

Chafetz Chayyim

Growing into a Relationship

Background: While others may not always understand why one person is attracted to another, even when we choose our own spouse, we have to grow into the relationship.

One has to be careful not to socialize with those who commit sins without giving such actions a second thought. These people are likely to lead even a good person astray, away from the ways of God, thrusting that person from the path of Torah (God forbid!) until that person becomes one of them. While you may feel always in control, not believing that anyone could lead you from living a decent life, you are wrong. You can be led astray.

Listen to this parable: A king's daughter was once taken captive and forced to marry an uncouth peasant boy. For a while, the young woman suffered intensely. She was so unfamiliar and uncomfortable with the behavior he had learned on the street. She was used to living in comfort, eating gourmet foods, and dressing in fine clothing.

Her home had been palatial and now she was forced to live in a hovel. She couldn't even eat the coarse food her husband had for his meals. She cried bitterly over her fate, thinking that death would be better than such a life.

But time has its own way of working, and eventually she grew accustomed to this new way of life. After a few years passed, one was unable to detect in this peasant woman the young refined princess she had once been.

Chafetz Chayyim

The Modesty of a Woman

Background: This talmudic story expresses the rabbinic
virtue of modesty in a marital relationship.

There was once a man who married a woman who had a
stump for one hand, but the man never noticed the deformity until the day she died.

Rabbi said, "How modest this woman must have been
that her husband was never able to notice her deformity."

Rabbi Hiyya said to him, "It was natural for her to hide
her hand, but how modest this man must have been, for
he never once examined his wife's body."

Babylonian Talmud, *Shabbat* 53b

The Weasel and the Pit

Background: This story, based on one in the Talmud, presents an interesting look at a marriage that dissolved and later reconstituted itself.

Once a well-dressed and very pretty young woman lost her way home. She wandered and wandered in the fields, finally becoming too exhausted to move any farther. Suddenly, she saw a well to which were attached a rope and bucket. To try to get at the water, she slid down the rope but was unable to pull herself up again. She cried and cried and finally attracted the attention of a young passerby who offered to help her if she promised to marry him. Although this was a very strange request, she did finally agree to marry him, and the young man pulled her out of the well.

Since there were no witnesses to testify to this marriage, which is required by Jewish law, the girl suggested that the well and a weasel that was seen near it would be called as witnesses. This was done, and the newly married couple parted.

The young woman remained faithful to her pledge of marriage, but the young man did not and left her. He married another woman, who bore him a son. At the age of three, the boy was choked to death by a weasel. Later, a second boy was born to the couple, and he fell into a well and was drowned. The mother was now alarmed by the peculiar nature of these happenings, and she urged her husband to offer an explanation.

Her husband told her the story of how he broke his promise to his former bride. After hearing this, his wife became very angry and demanded a divorce, which was granted to her. During all of that time, his former wife was waiting for his appearance, discouraging all her suitors by simulating epileptic fits. When the young man, after some searching, finally returned to her, she did not recognize him. She tried to fend him off, but when he mentioned the weasel and the well, she accepted him at once and they were happily remarried.

Based on Babylonian Talmud, *Taanit* 8a

Bet Hillel and Bet Shammai

Background: This story describes the famous dispute between the conservative school of Shammai and the more flexible school of Hillel about how to describe an unattractive bride. It has been the basis for many scholarly works on the subject of telling "white" lies. The lesson that is derived from this debate is that there are indeed times when it is often more important—and morally correct—to avoid hurting another person's feelings than to be totally truthful.

Our rabbis once wanted to know what one says to a bride if asked how she looks. Bet Shammai said, "Never exaggerate, but always give your truthful opinion." To which Bet Hillel said, "We disagree! Always tell a bride that she is graceful and beautiful!"

Bet Shammai then asked Bet Hillel, "If the bride were lame or blind, would you still say to her that 'you are graceful and beautiful'? Don't you know that even the Torah says to 'keep from telling lies'!"

Bet Hillel then answered Shammai by saying, "According to your own words, if one has made a bad purchase in the marketplace, should one praise it in his eyes or deprecate it? Surely one should praise it in his eyes." Therefore, the sages have said, "The disposition of a person should always be pleasant before people."

Babylonian Talmud, *Ketubot* 16b

Going to School: Rabbi Akiba Gets a Late Start

Background: Rabbi Akiba, an important talmudic sage, is most known for his late start in getting a Jewish education. This story describes the beginning of his Jewish odyssey.

How did Rabbi Akiba venture into Jewish studies? It is told that when he was forty years old he had not studied even one single thing. Once, he was standing by a well and asked, "Who cut a hole in this rock?" Students playing near the well answered, "The water that kept falling on it every day. Don't you know the verse 'Water wears away even stones'?"

Rabbi Akiba then began to reason to himself, "If something that is soft can wear down something that is hard, then certainly the words of Torah, which are hard as iron, can penetrate into my heart, which is only flesh and blood."

He and his son then went to a teacher of young children and said, "My teacher, teach me Torah!" Rabbi Akiba held one end of the slate and his son the other. The teacher wrote "*aleph bet*" for him, and Rabbi Akiba learned it. The teacher then wrote "*aleph tav*" for him, and he learned it. The teacher next wrote the book of Leviticus for him, and he learned it. He went on studying and eventually learned the entire Torah.

Rabbi Akiba then went and sat before Rabbi Eliezer and Rabbi Yehoshua, saying to them, "My teachers, teach me the meaning of the *Mishnah*." When they told him a specific law, he would go and sit by himself and ask himself, "This *aleph*, why is it written? This *bet*, why is it written?" He would then return to his teachers and ask them his questions, but his inquiries reduced them to silence.

It was Rabbi Shimon ben Elazar who then said, "I will explain Rabbi Akiba's study by means of a parable. To what can it be likened? To a stonecutter who was hacking away in the mountains. One time he took up his pickax and sat up on the mountain, chipping away at the mountain, tiny pebble by tiny pebble. People came by and said, "What are you doing?" He replied, "I am going to uproot this mountain and toss it into the Jordan River."

They said, "Impossible! You can't uproot a whole mountain!" But he kept cutting away and cutting away, until he came to a huge rock. He crawled under it, uprooted it, and threw it into the Jordan, saying "This isn't your place—that is where you belong!" That is what Rabbi Akiba did with the instruction of Rabbi Eliezer and Rabbi Joshua.

Rabbi Akiba began to study Torah at age forty, and by age fifty-three he was teaching Torah to throngs of people!

Adapted from *Avot de Rabbi Natan*

Divorce

The Separation Feast

Background: This story from the *Midrash* emphasizes the importance of trying to save a Jewish marriage. In addition, it emphasizes the power of prayer and its ability to affect childbearing.

Once upon a time a certain woman in Tzidon was married, but the couple had no children. The two of them went to Rabbi Shimon bar Yochai and asked him for a divorce.

The rabbi said, "By your lives, just as you were married with a great feast, so too shall you begin your separation with a great feast."

The couple followed the rabbi's instructions and made a feast. During the meal the woman gave the man too much to drink. Following the meal, as he got sober he said, "My dear, take a close look at all of the valuable things in this house. Take the one thing that is most dear to you and return to your father's house."

What did she do? After he fell asleep, she told her servants to carry him on his bed to her father's house.

In the middle of the night, he awoke and asked, "My beloved, what am I doing in your father's house?"

She answered, "Didn't you say to me this evening, 'Take whatever is most precious to you and take it with you to your father's house?' There is nothing more precious to me in the whole wide world than you!"

They then went back to Rabbi Shimon bar Yochai, who prayed for them, and they did have children.

Song of Songs Rabbah 1:1

Maintaining Jewish Family

Background: According to traditional law, a man may divorce his wife for one of several reasons, including the inability to bear children. There are those among us who certainly do not respond to this aspect of Jewish law very favorably. This story illustrates the extent to which even those who are charged to maintain Jewish law are sensitive to its spirit—the maintenance of Jewish family. This story is a variation on the theme of the previous story.

There was once a woman in Sidon who had been married to her husband for ten years but had remained childless. As a result, he decided to divorce his wife. Consequently, he went to Rabbi Simeon ben Yochai for advice.

The rabbi attempted to dissuade the man from his determined task since he professed to love his wife. But the rabbi's efforts were in vain. So he decided to address the man: "You made a feast when you were married. Thus, it is my advice that you should also separate good friends after a banquet."

The couple followed the rabbi's advice and caused a feast to be prepared at which the wife encouraged the husband to drink a lot of wine. "My dear," he said to the spouse he was about to leave, "take the most precious things out of the house with you before you leave."

So what did the woman do? When her husband was fast asleep, she asked her servants to carry him—still in his bed—to her parents' home. When the man awoke in the middle of the night to unfamiliar surroundings, he asked with surprise, "Where am I?" To which his wife replied, "You are in my parents' house."

"And what am I doing in your parents' home? How did I get here?" asked the man, astonished.

"I have acted according to your own instructions," replied the spouse sweetly. "Last night, you told me to take the most precious things from our home, but there is nothing more precious to me than you."

The husband was greatly moved, and in the morning they went together to see Rabbi Simeon ben Yochai in order to ask the rabbi to pray with them that a child be born—which it was.

Based on *Song of Songs Rabbah* 1:1

After So Many Years

Background: We often wonder how people can seek a divorce after many years of marriage. In a facetious sort of way, this story offers us some insight.

An older man came to his rabbi in order to divorce his wife. Surprised, the rabbi inquired of the man, "How old are you?" The fellow replied, "I am seventy." The rabbi pressed onward, "How long have you been married?" "Fifty years," came the response. The dialogue continued: "And how many children do you have?" "I have five sons and five daughters," the man proudly told the rabbi. "Are they married?" came the next question. "Yes," the man replied. Finally, the rabbi asked, "If you, as an old man, have been living with your wife for fifty years, and are the proud father of ten married children, why on earth do you want to now divorce your wife?"

"Well," said the man in reply, "I discovered on the day that I married my wife that she was lazy, selfish, and quite quarrelsome. But you know how it is. I soon learned that she was pregnant. Had I divorced her under such circumstances, it would have killed her. Her parents suggested to me, therefore, that I wait at least until after the child was born. So I waited.

"Following the birth of the child, there were celebrations and ceremonies of all sorts. What would people have thought of me had I sought a divorce in the midst of all that? So I waited a little longer.

"Then I found out that my wife was pregnant again and, for a period of time, I had to abandon all thoughts of divorce. This went on for many years. She was either preg-

nant or nursing. Had I divorced her under those circumstances, people would have thought that I was a beast.

"After our last child was born, I thought about it again.
This time, people said, 'What kind of a person are you?
You would leave ten children to grow up without a father?'
So I decided to wait until my children were grown up.

"When I finally announced my intention–after all of
our children had grown up–I was denounced. I was told
that such an action would impair my children's chances
for marriage. So I decided to wait until they were all married. Well, rabbi, they are all married and here I am."

Source unknown

Conversion

The Conversion of Terach

Background: This *midrash* attempts to help us understand how Abraham was able to convince his father, Terach, an idol maker, that building and creating idols was a useless profession.

Abraham's family were makers and sellers of idols. One day when it was Abraham's turn to sell idols in the marketplace, his father, Terach, filled a basket with them and sent him off to the market. Soon a man came to the stall and asked Abraham, "Do you have an idol to sell me that is big and strong?"

Abraham gave him the biggest idol he had in his store. As the man was about to leave the premises, Abraham asked, "How old are you?"

"I am a man of seventy years," said the man.

Then Abraham exclaimed, "You are a foolish man. At the age of seventy, you are prepared to bow down to an idol that was made only this morning!" The man immediately threw the idol into a garbage heap, took his money back, and ran off.

A few minutes later, a poor woman came into the store and inquired about purchasing a lowly idol. Abraham gave her the lowliest idol, and as she was about to leave Abraham asked her, "How old are you?"

"Very old," answered the woman.

"You foolish lady," said Abraham. "You have lived for many years and are willing to pray to an idol that was made only this morning."

The woman then put the idol back, retrieved her money, and went on her way.

Abraham continued to meet customers all throughout the day. Each time he convinced his customers to take their money back and not buy the idols.

At the end of the day a woman came into the store carrying a sack of flour. "Here," she said. "Give it to the idol gods." Abraham took a large stick, smashed all the idols in his store except for the largest one, and placed the stick in the hand of the largest idol. When his father, Terach, returned home and asked what happened, Abraham said, "Look, I cannot tell a lie. A woman came and gave me some flour as an offering to our idols. As I put the food down, each idol came and demanded the food for himself. Then the largest one took a hammer and smashed all the others!"

With this Terach replied, "You are making a fool of me. Idols cannot speak, nor can they move."

"Let my father's ears hear what his mouth says," Abraham replied in a quiet tone.

Various traditional sources

The Cow Who Rested on Shabbat

Background: This talmudic story reminds the reader that traditional Jews not only rest on *Shabbat* but allow their animals to rest as well. It also attempts to show how this concept can influence a non-Jewish person to convert to Judaism.

Eliezer owned a very special cow. Not only was it a hard worker all during the week, but when it came to the Sabbath, it rested! The cow worked for Eliezer for many years.

Time passed, and after several difficult years resulting in small harvests, Eliezer was forced to sell his beloved cow to a non-Jew.

During the first few days of the new ownership, the cow worked and plowed with as much diligence as it had for its previous owner. Finally, when the seventh day arrived, the holy Sabbath, the cow would not allow itself to be hitched to the plow. The new owner yelled all kinds of commands to her: "Go, move, forward, march!" but the cow would not move even a single inch.

Angrily, the new owner ran to Eliezer's house. "What kind of a cow did you try and sell me? She won't work anymore. I want all of my money back!"

"I simply do not understand," said Eliezer. "She was always a hard and faithful worker for me. Take me to her and we shall see what seems to be the problem."

The two men walked over to the field where the cow lay on the grassy field.

"Does she look like a worker to you?" screamed the new owner. "She won't even move from her place."

Eliezer bent down and whispered something into the cow's ear. Suddenly the cow rose, prepared to work again!

"What did you say to her?" the new owner asked.

"I told her that when she belonged to me, we all rested on the holy Sabbath, as God had instructed us. But now she belongs to a new owner, who is not Jewish and who does not rest on the Sabbath. So she must now learn to work on the Sabbath as he does."

The new owner paused and then said, "If an animal can learn to listen to God and rest on the Sabbath, I believe I can too." So he took the cow back to his barn and said that he never would work her again on the Sabbath. Soon he began to study Jewish laws and became more and more interested in Judaism. It was not long before he officially became a Jew, and later a rabbi as well. He was known as Rabbi Hanina ben Torta, the rabbi who was the son of a cow!

Asseret Hadibrot; Pesikta Rabbati, chapter 14

Onkelos' Conversion to Judaism

Background: Onkelos, the nephew of Emperor Titus, converted to Judaism and became a true scholar. One of his greatest achievements was his translation of the Torah into Aramaic, the *lingua franca* of the time. Now everyone could understand it.

When Caesar heard that Onkelos had converted to Judaism, he sent messengers to have him returned to Rome. But Onkelos, a man of great charisma, taught Torah to the messengers, and they too joined him in his new faith!

Again Caesar sent messengers to Onkelos, this time instructing them not to engage in any debate lest they too embrace Judaism. When the new messengers arrived, Onkelos asked them this one question: "When the master of the house walks in a dark street, who lights his way?"

The messengers replied, "His slave."

To which Onkelos responded, "This is not the case with the God of Israel. When the Israelite slaves left Egypt and wandered through the desert, God lit their way with the cloud of glory by day and the pillar of fire by night."

When the messengers heard this story, they embraced Judaism!

Word got back to Caesar about the fate of his second group of messengers. This time Caesar was more furious than ever. Again, he decided to dispatch a third set of messengers to Onkelos. This time, he warned them not to speak even a single word to him.

When they finally arrived, Onkelos placed his hand on the *mezuzah* in his doorway.

"What is that?" asked the messengers.

"Let me ask you this question first," answered Onkelos. "When a king enters his house, who guards the door?"

"His servants," the messengers replied.

Onkelos then responded, "The exact opposite is true of the God of the Jewish people. The Sovereign of all Sovereigns guards our door while we, God's servants, remain safely inside. Our God loves us that much!"

Hearing this, the third group of messengers embraced Judaism and became Jews.

When Caesar heard this, he decided that he would never again send any more messengers to Onkelos.

Babylonian Talmud, *Avodah Zarah* 11a

God Loves the Proselyte

Background: This story is a polemic against those who hold to the opinion that persons converting to Judaism are not to be held in as great esteem as persons born into Judaism. This story tells us that God loves proselytes!

More dear to God is the proselyte who has come of her own accord than are the crowds of Israelites who stood before Mount Sinai. For had the Israelites not witnessed the thunder, lightning, quaking mountain, and sounding trumpets at Mount Sinai, they would not have accepted the Torah. But the proselyte, who did not see these things, who came and surrendered herself to God and took the yoke of heaven upon herself, and accepted the commandments, can anyone be dearer to God than this person?

Tanchuma, *Lech Lecha* 6, f.32a

The Repulsion of Timna

Background: Unlike liberal Judaism, traditional Judaism does not initially encourage the individual to convert to Judaism. However, once a person has made the decision to convert, that person is to be welcomed into the community and not reminded of his or her non-Jewish past. This talmudic story explains that evil can result when one does not welcome a proselyte into Judaism.

Once upon a time there was a princess named Timna. She wanted to convert to Judaism. So she went to Abraham, Isaac, and Jacob, but they would not receive her. She then became a concubine of Eliphaz, the son of Esau, for she said, "It is better to become a handmaid of this nation than a princess of any other." Her son was Amalek, who would bring a great deal of trouble to Israel. Why was this so? Because they should not have repelled her.

Babylonian Talmud, *Sanhedrin* 99b

Becoming a Jew

Background: This talmudic story provides us with a prism through which to look into the minds of the rabbis as they discussed the procedure for conversion many centuries ago.

Our rabbis said, "If anyone comes nowadays and desires to convert to Judaism, they say to him, 'Why do you want to become a proselyte? Don't you know that the Israelites these days are persecuted and harassed?'

"If the person says, 'I know it and I am not worthy,' they receive him at once and explain to him some of the different kinds of religious instructions and tell him of the sins connected with the laws of gleaning, the forgotten sheaf, and the tithe for the poor.

"When they tell him of the punishments they also tell him of the rewards, saying to him that the World to Come has been created for the righteous people. They do not, however, tell him too many details. If he agrees to everything, then they circumcise him, immerse him in the mikveh, and tell him of the various Jewish laws. After immersion in the mikveh, he is regarded in all respects as an Israelite!"

Babylonian Talmud, Yevamot 47a–b

Akilas Becomes a Jew

Background: Akilas was known for his fine translation of the Bible into Greek. This story from the *midrash* explains how Akilas, an eventual disciple of Rabbi Akiba, became a Jew.

Akilas once said to Hadrian Caesar, "I want to convert and become Jewish."

Hadrian angrily replied, "You would join this people that I have humiliated and that I have slain? What do you see in such people that would want to make you become Jewish?"

Akilas answered, "The least among them knows how God created the world, what was created on each of the days, and how the world was founded. Besides, their Torah is truth."

Hadrian then said, "Go ahead and study their Torah, but do not be circumcised."

Akilas said, "Unless he is circumcised, even the wisest person in the kingdom cannot study their Torah, concerning which it is said, 'God declares the divine word to Jacob, statutes and laws to Israel. God does not accord these to any other nation' (Psalm 147:19–20). To what nation alone does God give *mitzvot*? To the people of Israel."

Exodus Rabbah 30:12

Hillel and the Pagan

Background: Hillel and Shammai were two rabbinic contemporaries. Hillel was known for his more lenient positions, while Shammai was known for his rigor and stringency. This talmudic story relates how Rabbi Hillel was able to embrace and reach out to a heathen, convincing him to become a Jew.

Many years ago there lived two famous rabbis—one was Shammai and the other was Hillel. Shammai became easily angered when someone did not conduct himself properly. Hillel, on the other hand, was more lenient and patient, and rarely became angry.

Once a heathen came to Shammai and said, "I want to become Jewish. But I make one condition. You must teach me the entire Torah while I stand on one foot!"

When Shammai heard this, he became angry at the man's foolishness. How could it be possible for any person to learn the whole Torah while standing on one foot, he thought to himself. Shammai then took a long stick and chased the heathen from his house.

Next, the heathen went to Rabbi Hillel. "I want to become a Jew," he said, "but on condition that you teach me the whole Torah while I stand on one foot!"

To this Hillel answered, "Good, I accept your challenge."

The heathen stood on one foot and Hillel taught him, "Whatever is hateful to you, never do to your fellow person. This is the whole Torah. The rest is commentary. Now go and learn all of the laws so that you will know what to do and what not to do."

The heathen listened to Hillel's words. He studied the Torah and became a very good Jew.

Babylonian Talmud, *Shabbat* 31a

The Power of the Tallit

Background: This talmudic legend explains the power of the *tallit* as a symbol of God's commandments. The *tallit* and its fringes (*tzitzit*) can even give a person the strength to overcome his *yetzer hara* in the form of illicit passion.

There was once a young scholar who was especially knowledgeable and scrupulous in his observance of the laws of *tzitzit*. Once he heard about a very beautiful harlot who lived in a distant land. His passion got the best of him, so he set off to see her in person. As soon as he arrived at her house, he paid her a fee of four hundred golden dinarim and was invited in. He entered her bedroom, only to see her lying naked on the bed. She was voluptuous. He began to undress when suddenly the *tzitzit* on his *tallit katan* flew up and struck him in the face. At that point, he turned away from the prostitute and sat down on the floor.

The woman came down from the bed and inquired whether he had found fault with her. He gently told her that she was the most beautiful woman he had ever seen. And then he told her about his *tzitzit*.

The woman said to him, "I will not let you go until you write down your name, the name of your hometown, your school's name, and the name of your teacher on this paper." When the young scholar left, she sold her possessions, gave a third of her money to charity, and went to Jerusalem. There she visited her visitor's teacher, Rabbi Chiyya, and said, "Convert me."

Rabbi Chiyya was immediately taken by her beauty. He was surprised and puzzled. "Have you fallen in love with one of my students?" he asked.

The woman did not answer. Instead, she gave Chiyya the note that the student had given to her. Rabbi Chiyya read the note and immediately recognized the handwriting of his pupil. He converted the woman and then arranged for her to marry his young disciple.

Babylonian Talmud, *Menachot* 44a

IV
THE
OLDER
YEARS

Even in old age, they shall bring forth fruit.

Psalm 92:15

Because of extended life expectancy and improved health care, there are more older adults alive today than at any other time in the history of humankind. We rejoice in the blessing of old people. While Judaism is realistic about the challenges of growing older, sacred Jewish texts generally praise old age and speak in positive metaphor about it. For old age represents the ideal age for Judaism. With old age comes the greatest potential for wisdom. This is unlike the negative tendency of contemporary culture in Western civilization. Honor and respect that are due older people are very important for the Bible and rabbinic literature. Listen to the words of Rabbi Yose bar Yehudah, who wrote in *Pirke Avot* (4:26), "The one who learns from the young may be likened to one who eats unripe grapes and drinks wine from the vat. But the person who learns from the old may be likened to one who eats ripe grapes and drinks wine that is aged."

In this section of the book, which we call The Older Years, we include stories dealing with such themes as parenting in old age, the secret of reaching old age, and traditional views of the elderly patriarch Abraham and the famous Rabbi Akiba. Perhaps in them you will see people you know, even members of your own family.

143

Going to Extremes

Background: Many of the *mitzvot* associated with the honor and respect due older people emanate from the basic instruction to honor one's parents. In this tale, Rabbi Tarfon goes to an extreme in order to fulfill it.

Rabbi Tarfon always paid special attention to the fulfillment of the *mitzvah kibud av ve'em* (the honoring of parents). He visited his elderly mother daily and did chores for her around the house. She would beg him, "Tarfon, it is not dignified for you to do these chores. Let me hire a servant to do it. You are a great teacher who should not lower himself to such menial tasks."

Tarfon gently replied to his mother, "Do you think that I consider these chores menial? I consider helping you the greatest honor I can offer." They would argue this way back and forth; it became a sort of loving game for the two of them.

One *Shabbat*, when Tarfon came to visit his mother, he found her stopped in the street, refusing to move. "What's the matter, Mother?" he inquired. "Oh, it's nothing," came the reply. "My shoe strap broke, and I am afraid to walk. I do not want to injure my feet." Since it was *Shabbat*, he could not fetch his mother another pair of shoes. Instead, he reached down and placed his hand under her foot. "What are you doing?" queried his mother, rather surprised at his peculiar behavior. "I do not want you to walk barefoot. Step on my hand so that I might help you home," came the reply. Tarfon accompanied his mother home in this manner.

Once when Tarfon was ill, his friends came to visit

him. His mother begged them to pray for his recovery. His friends asked how Tarfon had honored her. So she related to them the story of the broken sandal. The friends asked, "Do you think that he has fulfilled the entire *mitzvah* of *kibud av ve'em* toward you?" "Oh, no," came the reply. "Even if he showed me even more honor, he would not come close to fulfilling even half of the requirements of that *mitzvah*. You see, such a *mitzvah* has no limit at all."

Based on Jerusalem Talmud, *Pe'ah*

Living Up to
the Responsibility

Background: The responsibility to care for one's parents when they grow old is one of the core issues regarding the individual's responsibility for the aged. As this tale indicates, some people do not always live up to their obligations.

Once an old man who could no longer care for himself went to live with his son. The son fed him daily, but he loathed the task he had to perform. The old man could see the disgust in his son's face. He wondered how his son could afford to feed him so well, but he did not want to inquire. Finally, he could contain himself no longer. "How can you afford to continue to feed me this way?"

"Silence," came the son's insensitive reply. "You must eat like a dog eats whatever is placed before you." This is what the sages meant when they said, "A person can feed one's parent fattened fowl and still deserve *Gehinnom*."

Based on Jerusalem Talmud, *Pe'ah*

The Servant Who
Dyed His Hair

Background: This talmudic story reflects an incident in the life of an older man who dyed his hair black in order to attempt to gain employment. (Using hair coloring for purposes of deception was expressly forbidden in talmudic times.)

An old man dyed his hair black and came to Rabba saying, "Buy me!"

Rabba answered, "I have enough servants in my household."

The man then went to Rab Papa bar Samuel, who accepted him as a servant. Thereupon the servant washed his head and beard white again and said to him, "See, I am older than your father."

Rab Papa could not ask such an old man to be his servant.

Babylonian Talmud, *Bava Metzia* 60b

Planting in Old Age

Background: This story demonstrates the important Jewish value of planting seeds for future generations.

Once, Emperor Hadrian noticed an old man planting a fig tree. He halted his horse and asked him, "Why, old man, are you working so diligently to plant that tree? Surely you do not expect to see the fruits of your labors?"

The old man replied, "If it be God's will that I eat the figs, then so be it. If not, my sons will enjoy them."

Three years passed and the emperor again passed the old man's garden. The same old man approached Hadrian with a basket of figs and, handing it to him, said, "Please accept this gift. I am the person to whom you spoke three years ago."

The emperor was deeply moved and directed his servants to fill the basket with gold coins to be given to the man.

The wife of this man's neighbor heard the story of the gold coins and immediately told her husband to go to the emperor with a basket of fruit. She hoped that her husband's basket would also be filled with gold coins.

The husband followed his wife's instructions and brought the fruit basket to the emperor. "Sir," he said, "this basket of fruit is for you for your personal enjoyment."

On hearing the story, the emperor became very angry at the man's boldness and ordered his soldiers to throw food in his face. Bruised and almost blinded, the trickster returned to his home.

His wife asked, "Well, how did you do?"

Her husband replied, "Had I taken *etrogim*, I would have died from the blows."

Leviticus Rabbah 25

The Elderly Rabbi Akiba

Background: In this story we see how scrupulous was Rabbi Akiba in his observance of Jewish law. With little water to drink while in prison, Rabbi Akiba used it for the ritual washing of hands.

When Rabbi Akiba was in prison, only a limited amount of water was brought to him each day. One day, Rabbi Joshua, Akiba's disciple, was asked by the prison warden, "Why is your water today set above the usual limit? Do you require that much to breach the prison walls?"

Hearing this, the warden poured out half of the water and left the other half. When Rabbi Joshua came in to Rabbi Akiba, Rabbi Akiba said to him, "Joshua, do you know that I am an old man and that my life depends on yours? Why are you so late?"

Rabbi Joshua told him all that had happened. Rabbi Akiba then said, "Give me some water to wash my hands." Rabbi Joshua replied, "The water I brought you is not even enough for drinking. How can it be used for washing your hands?"

Rabbi Akiba answered, "What else am I to do? I would rather starve myself to death than disregard the opinion of my colleagues and not wash my hands."

Rabbi Akiba did not drink until Rabbi Joshua managed to bring him more water with which to wash his hands. When the sages heard of this incident, they said, "If he is so careful in his old age, how much more careful he must have been in his youth. And if Akiba behaves in this manner in prison, how much more careful he must be in his own home!"

Babylonian Talmud, *Eruvin* 21b

The Elderly Abraham

Background: In this legend, old age is described as a mark of distinction.

Until the time of Abraham, young persons and old persons were not distinguishable one from the other. A person could live to be several hundred years old and not bear any of the signs of aging.

Once Abraham said to God, "*Adonai*, Sovereign of the Universe, there must be an outward sign that You will provide for a father and a son or between young and old persons." God listened and said to Abraham, "I will begin with you."

Abraham went into a deep sleep and when he awakened the very next morning, he saw that his hair and beard had turned white. Turning toward God he said, "Sovereign of the Universe, You have made me an example."

Tanchuma, *Chayyei Sarah*, paragraph 1

Parenting in Old Age

Background: It is difficult enough to raise children when you are young. It is even more difficult to raise them as you grow older. But the responsibility of parenting never ceases, says this tale, even as children grow into adulthood.

A long time ago, a son was born to a man in his old age in the city of Jerusalem. When the boy had reached the age of six and was old enough to begin to understand the meaning of things and to distinguish between good and evil, his father, noticing these gifts of discernment, decided to keep him away from the frivolous things in the world. He raised him in the study of Torah so that he would gain life in this world and in the World to Come. "My child," thought the old man, "will be the joy and honor of my own old age."

So the old man locked up the boy in a special apartment that he shared with a famous and learned teacher whom the old man had engaged as sole tutor for his son. Day and night they studied, and in order to prevent the boy from being distracted by the wonders and pleasures of the world, anything the boy wanted was brought to the apartment. The master teacher was given all that he desired as well. They remained in seclusion like this for ten years, studying God's Holy Law. The young boy soon acquired a vast knowledge of Scripture.

Years passed and the father grew even older while the son matured into adulthood. One day, the old man said to himself, "My end is near and soon I will have to return to my Maker the pledge I have received. What shall I do with all my possessions after I am gone? Should the toil of my hands be lost? My only son is ignorant of the ways of the world and unacquainted with the intricacies of the marketplace. Should my wealth be lost and one day my son be driven to the necessity of reaching out his hand like a beggar?"

These thoughts troubled the old man. And so he began to teach his son the affairs of business. The son would accompany him on business trips and quickly developed a keen knowledge of commerce.

"Be careful," the old man warned his son. "Do not abandon God's ways, for happy is the one who can combine the ways of life with the ways of Torah." Thus spoke the father to his son. And the son was receptive to all that his father taught him. Shortly thereafter, the old man died, going the way of all flesh.

As soon as the days of mourning were over, the son collected all the treasures and money that his father had left him and went to travel the world. He visited many cities until he came to the capital of Turkey. One day, when he was walking through the streets, he came upon—in the open square—an iron coffin suspended from an iron chain between two pillars. The coffin was guarded by a soldier. The traveler's curiosity was aroused and he tried to query the guard, only to be told to mind his own business. "Go on," ordered the soldier. "Don't meddle in things that do not concern you." The young man was not quickly dissuaded and offered the guard a handful of silver in exchange for the information he sought.

"This coffin," said the suddenly friendly guard, "contains the body of a Jew who, during his lifetime, was the financial adviser to the sultan. He managed the sultan's treasury, and the sultan trusted and respected him. But one day, his enemies, envious of his success, conspired against him and convinced the ruler that his financial adviser had poorly administered his funds and was subverting them for his own benefit. They said that he had robbed the sultan of large sums of money. They succeeded in poisoning the sultan's mind. Consequently, the sultan summoned his treasurer and required him to provide him with complete and detailed records of all transactions during the twenty years he had been in the sultan's service.

"The Jewish banker became frightened. How could he remember twenty years' worth of transactions? Vainly, he pleaded his own innocence, but the irate ruler would not listen. Convinced that he had been cheated and robbed, he condemned his former adviser to death and ordered that he should be embalmed and kept this way until the Jewish community repaid his debt. And so, here the coffin remains."

Genuinely moved by the story, and finding out how much money the sultan sought, the young man requested an audience with the king. With these words, he addressed the sultan: "I have come from a distant land and I am ready to repay the claimed sum as ransom for this poor banker. If it please you, set the body free so that it might be buried according to the custom of the Jewish community."

Glad to have his money back, the sultan set the body free with instructions that it might be buried in accordance with Jewish law. But the generous youth was not satisfied. He asked the sultan yet one more favor: "If it please your majesty, may it be decreed that all of the inhabitants of the city be present at the funeral, young and old alike." The sultan graciously agreed and issued the requested decree.

But on the following day, the sultan summoned the stranger and offered to return his money in exchange for a celestial award that would be awaiting the young man in return for his noble deed. But the young man refused. He said, "I am your slave and your obedient servant, but this I cannot do. What good is a person if that person does not use all he has at his disposal to fulfill God's instructions? All my life I yearned for an opportunity to fulfill this obligation. How can I now bargain it away?"

The sultan deferred to the stranger and let him go in peace. The young man left the capital of Turkey and, after continuing his journey somewhat farther, eventually made his way home. But shortly after he boarded a ship that was to take him home, a storm plummeted the ship and cast into the sea all of its passengers, who quickly drowned— except for the young man. Seeing a plank in the distance, he swam to it and clung to it until he finally drifted safely to shore. There he sat down and burst into tears. He was far from home, his possessions lost at sea. He was destitute.

Suddenly a white eagle swooped down and addressed the traveler in what appeared to be the language of the birds. While the young man could not understand the language of the bird, he assumed that the eagle was a messenger from God. When the great bird spread its wings, he climbed on. It brought him to Jerusalem and then disappeared. In the darkness of night, the traveler beheld a man wrapped in a white shroud and was frightened. But the white shroud spoke to him: "Do not be afraid. I am the dead banker for whom you performed a noble deed. I appeared to you as a plank of wood and as an eagle in order to save you from certain death. Now be happy, for you will enjoy this life and know that a reward awaits you in the next."

And the honest boy was happy until the end of his life and never neglected the study of Torah or the opportunity to do good deeds.

Shaarei Yerushalayim and *Sefer Hamassiyot*

The Secret of Reaching Old Age

Background: This talmudic story attempts to unlock the mystery of why some people reach a ripe old age.

Rabbi Nechunia ben HaKaneh was asked by his students, "By virtue of what have you reached such a good old age?"

He replied, "Never in my life have I sought respect through the degradation of my fellow, nor has the curse of my fellow gone up with me upon my bed, and I have been generous with my money."

Rabbi Judah the Prince asked Rabbi Joshua ben Korcha, "By virtue of what have you reached such a good old age?"

He replied, "Never in my life have I gazed at the countenance of a wicked man."

Rabbi Zera was asked by his students, "By virtue of what have you reached such a good old age?" He replied, "Never in my life have I been harsh with my household, nor have I stepped in front of one greater than myself, nor have I meditated on the Torah in dirty alleys, nor have I gone four cubits without Torah and without *tefillin*, nor have I slept in the *Bet Hamidrash*, either a long or a short sleep, nor have I rejoiced in the downfall of my fellow humans, nor have I called my fellow by his nickname."

Babylonian Talmud, *Megillah* 28a

V

THE
FINAL
YEARS

The dust returns to the earth as it was, but the spirit returns to God who gave it.

Ecclesiastes 3:2

For some, the prospect of death is frightening. For others, it comes as the natural end to a life well lived. While we all consider the challenge of our own finitude, we have to face death just the same. We have no alternatives. Thus, just as there is a Jewish way of life, so too is there a Jewish way of death. Through its traditions, Judaism expresses a realistic attitude toward death. Its laws about mourning and bereavement are built into a community structure that is designed to provide the individual with stability and support while faced with the pain following the death of a loved one.

Traditional Jewish belief views the world in which we live as a corridor that leads to another world. The belief in an afterlife, in a World to Come, where people are judged—while their souls are given the opportunity for eternal life—is embedded deeply in Jewish thought. The details are scattered throughout Jewish literature and there is no one Jewish position, but it is part of mainstream Jewish tradition nonetheless.

These stories, dealing with the struggle of a person's final years, present us with a variety of themes. These tales include such elements as the Angel of Death, last-minute advice, how we die, the death of children, views of the World to Come, and the deaths of well-known personalities from the Bible and Talmud such as Adam, Jacob, Moses, Aaron, Rabbi Yochanan ben Zakkai, King David, Absalom, and Rabbi Zusya of Hanipol.

Last-Minute Advice

Background: This is a story of one father's attempt to provide his son with worldly advice, even as he takes leave of this world.

There was once a pious man, held in high esteem by all, who had a son who was both handsome and noble. When the time came for him to die, the father summoned his son and instructed him never to leave a place of worship before the *shaliach hatzibbur* had recited all of the prayers and the entire service had been completed. He also advised his son to enter the synagogue whenever he heard the prayers of the cantor from the street and remain there until the service was over.

The pious man died and the son found favor in everyone's eyes and soon became the chief steward of the royal household. He served the wine and filled the glasses. He cut bread and carved meat. He enjoyed the favor of the ruler but remained true to God and never forgot his father's teachings. But the king's chief of staff was jealous of the chief steward and sought to undermine him in the eyes of the king. At first, the king refused to believe what his own chief of staff was telling him, but he eventually believed him. He became enraged and vengeful about what he was told.

One day, as he was passing by the lime quarry that was prepared for construction, he told the foreman that the first person to appear as his messenger in the morning should be placed in the kiln and put to death. The foreman replied, "I will obey your command."

In the evening, the boy served the king as usual and the king said to him, "Get up early tomorrow morning and

165

go to the lime quarry and tell the foreman to heat the kilns hotter than normal." Unsuspecting, the boy accepted his task with great honor. He got up early the next morning and rode to the quarry, but on his way he heard a reader in one of the local synagogues chanting the morning service. He dismounted and entered the synagogue and remained until the service was completed, at which time he mounted his horse to complete his task.

In the meantime, the king had summoned his chief of staff and asked him to go to the lime quarry in order to make sure that the foreman did what he had been told. As soon as the chief of staff appeared, he was seized and thrown into the kiln. At that moment, the boy arrived and was astonished to see what was happening. "The king will make you suffer for this horrible deed," he called out to the foreman. But the foreman merely shrugged his shoulders and said, "I have only done what the king ordered me to do."

The young boy returned to the king, who was, needless to say, surprised to see him. "Did you disobey me?" asked the king, whereupon the young boy reported what he had observed at the lime quarry.

Turning pale, the king said to the boy, "I see now that you are honest and God fearing and beloved of God. The chief of staff had spoken ill of you and in my anger, I believed him. I sent you to the lime quarry and then sent him after you to make sure that the foreman threw you into the oven. You tarried on your way and your accuser was killed in your stead. Truly the wise person said, 'The righteous is delivered out of trouble and the wicked come in his stead' [Proverbs 11:8]."

Various traditional sources

The Golden Box

Background: The material gifts one leaves one's children can often be the force that separates them from one another—even at the time they need each other most.

Once a pious man left to his three sons a locked golden box. They were told to open the box only in the case of a dire emergency. Each of the sons took a turn at keeping the key while another son kept the box in his possession. The three sons swore to obey their dead father's instruction, and they divided the inheritance he had left them evenly among themselves.

After a short period of time, the youngest son spent his entire inheritance and urged his brothers to open the box. The older brother said that he preferred to lend him money rather than disobey their father's wishes. A short time later, the youngest son reappeared and was penniless again. This time, the other brother followed the example of his older brother and lent the youngest brother some funds.

A short time passed and the third son found himself without funds once again. However, it was the young son's turn to guard the box. So he had a new key made and opened the box and stole all of the money it contained and quickly spent it on unnecessary frills. When it was the oldest brother's turn to guard the box, the youngest brother came to him and said, "I am again penniless and have no luck in business. I therefore urge you to open the box, since there is now an urgent need." The box was opened in the presence of witnesses and found to be empty. A stone had been placed in the box instead of the funds. The real thief accused the other brothers in the presence of witnesses: "You see, my brothers have taken all the money and left me destitute. That's why they refused to open the box." The witnesses advised the brothers to take their case to a learned rabbi who alone could unravel the mystery of the "stolen" funds.

On their way to see the rabbi, they encountered a man who inquired whether they had seen a horse that had been stolen from him. One brother asked, "Was it a white horse?" The man answered affirmatively. The brother responded, "Then you will find it in the woods." The second brother queried, "Was it blind in one eye?" And again the owner replied, "Yes." And the third brother inquired, "Was it carrying two casks, one of wine and one of oil?" And again the man replied, "Yes." He hurried into the woods in order to find his horse, but his search was fruitless. So he too went to the rabbi and accused the three brothers of stealing his horse.

"These three men have stolen my horse," he reported to the rabbi, "and all the gold and supplies it carried. They gave me an exact description of the horse." The first brother replied, "I knew that it was white on account of the hairs it had left on you." The second brother added, "We only guessed that it was blind in one eye and was carrying two flasks, one of wine and one of oil. We saw that the grass had been eaten only on one side of the road, and we noticed drips of oil and wine alongside." The rabbi found their responses plausible and dismissed the man to look for his horse.

Then he turned to the three brothers and asked each of them to tell him the story of the box and the disappearance of the funds from his own individual perspective. "But since you are all clever men, I want you to help me on a case submitted to me by one of my colleagues in Egypt. There were two wealthy men in Egypt. One man had a son, and the other man had a daughter. They decided that the two children should marry at the appropriate time. The parents of the couple died before the date of the marriage arrived, and each set of parents left to their child the sum of three hundred gold pieces. The woman was very virtuous, but the man was frivolous and quickly spent his inheritance. The woman was ready to enter into marriage, but the man refused, saying, 'Go marry someone else. I am unworthy.' Eventually, she met a young student with whom she fell in love and wanted to marry.

"The young woman told her new love that she was prepared to marry him but wanted him to visit his original fiancée in order to determine whether in fact he intended to marry her or not. In the interim, the woman dressed in silk and velvet and approached her original fiancé and repeated her offer to marry him. And the man refused, again telling her that he was unworthy. But the woman continued to make an effort to persuade the man whom her parents had wanted her to marry. Each time, she appeared to the man in more beautiful clothing, more expensive jewelry, and looked more beautiful. And again, the man released her from any obligation she felt. Finally, the woman accepted the man's refusal and married the poor student. On the way home from the wedding, they were mugged. Before the mugger could attempt to rape the bride, the groom persuaded him to let them go.

"And now," said the rabbi, "I must determine who acted more nobly than the others: the young man, the bride, or the mugger?"

"In my opinion," said the oldest brother, "the young man was the most noble since he released the woman from her responsibility to marry him."

"No," said the second brother, "the woman was nobler. She wanted to marry the student, yet continued to urge her first love to fulfill their obligation to their parents."

"You are both wrong," said the youngest brother. "The robber and potential rapist was the noblest since he sent the couple away without stealing her jewels and stopped before raping her."

The rabbi interrupted and said, "Praised is the God who reveals all secrets. You are guilty. You who coveted the money and jewels that you never saw could never resist the temptation to take the money in the box that was in your possession." In the end, the young man confessed to his deed.

Various traditional sources

Good Deeds Prevent Death

Background: Death is a mystery that eludes human comprehension and therefore we look for ways to prevent it. This story emphasizes the Jewish notion that the doing of good deeds can forestall death—but death is inevitable nonetheless.

A man named Ben Sabbar was always anxious to seize an opportunity to do a good deed. One day he heard about a poor girl who was about to be married but did not have the funds to do so. So he went to the neighboring town where the young woman lived and gave the woman all that he possessed. On his way home, he was inundated by a flood, but a nearby dragon changed itself into a bridge over which Ben Sabbar passed into safety. He continued on his way until he was stopped by a stranger.

"Are you Ben Sabbar?" asked the stranger. When Ben Sabbar responded positively, the stranger pushed further: "Your destiny is in my hand and your end is near." And so it was, for the stranger was none other than the Angel of Death. On hearing these words, Ben Sabbar grew pale and lifted his eyes to heaven, praying, "God of the Universe, shall I who have practiced charity die while I am still a young man? Is this the reward of virtue? Shall I die far from my home like some vile creature, without my family to pay me my last respects?"

A heavenly voice responded: "You have time to reach your home and lie down on your bed." And the Angel of Death left Ben Sabbar as he continued his journey home. When he encountered people on the way, he asked whether there was a local rabbi with whom he might speak. They told him of a Rabbi Shefifon ben Laish, and Ben Sabbar went to the rabbi, who greeted him warmly. Noticing how tense and anxious Ben Sabbar appeared, the rabbi asked whether Ben Sabbar was ill. And so Ben Sabbar related the story to the rabbi, who said, "Be of good cheer. God will protect you from the Angel of Death." Five days later, dark clouds appeared around the rabbi's house. The Angel of Death appeared and asked for its pledge. "Of what pledge are you speaking?" asked Rabbi Shefifon.

"Your life and the life of your guest, Ben Sabbar," responded the angel. The rabbi quickly uttered God's Name (YHWH), and the Angel of Death disappeared, only to take his case to the Creator of the Universe. "Master of the Universe," he complained, "Shefifon ben Laish refuses to obey Your decrees." But a heavenly voice proclaimed, "Pious people have the power to annul even the decrees of heaven." And God commanded the angels to add seventy years each to the lives of Ben Sabbar and Rabbi Shefifon.

Chibbur Massiyot

Seeing the Angel of Death

Background: Stories abound concerning the Angel of Death. This is one of many stories that attempt to describe the angel. If you know what she looks like, maybe you can avoid her when you see her, goes the logic.

The Angel of Death is said to be full of eyes. When the hour comes for a sick person to die, the Angel of Death positions itself above the head of the sick person with a sword drawn in the angel's hand. On the sword, a drop of gall dangles precariously. When the sick person sees the Angel of Death, the sick person trembles with fear and opens his or her mouth. At that point, the Angel of Death flicks a drop of gall into the sick person's mouth. From that drop, the sick person dies and the face turns green.

Babylonian Talmud, *Avodah Zarah* 20a

Returning to Tell the Story

Background: The stories of their teachers' deaths puzzled the rabbis. But they tried to learn from them nonetheless. In retelling these stories, they were comforted as well.

Rava was sitting in front of Rabbi Nachman as Rabbi Nachman was in the throes of death. Rabbi Nachman said to Rava, "Master, tell the Angel of Death not to torture me." Rava replied, "Master, are you not an important person [so that you might influence the Angel of Death yourself]"? Nachman responded, "Who is important, honored, or even respected by the Angel of Death?" Rava then continued, "Master, will you appear to me after your death?"

So he appeared to him and Rava asked Rabbi Nachman, "Master, did you suffer pain when your soul departed?" The answer, "It was like removing a hair from milk. But if the Holy Blessed One said to me, 'You can go back to the world,' I would not do so. That's how much I am afraid of the Angel of Death."

Babylonian Talmud, *Mo'ed Katan* 28a

Final Judgment

Background: We live our lives anticipating that we will eventually be judged for the way we led them. This story suggests that perhaps some people are "swept away without judgment."

Rav Joseph wept when he read the verse "But some are swept away without judgment" (Proverbs 13:23). He said to himself, "Is there anyone who is taken before his or her time?" Such is the case of Rav Bibi bar Abbaye, who had frequent contact with the Angel of Death.

Once, the Angel of Death said to its messenger, "Go, fetch me Miriam the women's hairstylist." So the messenger left and brought back Miriam the children's nurse. The angel said to the messenger, "I told you Miriam the hairstylist." The messenger responded, "Shall I take her back?" Now the angel replied, "Since you went to the trouble of bringing her, why not let her stay! But how were you able to overpower her?" The messenger responded, "She took a shovel in her hand and raked the oven. When she put the shovel on her knee, she burned herself. That's when her *mazal* was shaken, and I quickly brought her."

Rav Bibi Bar Abbaye said to the angel, "Do you have permission to act that way?" That's when the angel answered the rabbi, "Is it not written, 'Some are swept away without judgment.'"

Babylonian Talmud, *Chagigah* 4b–5a

King David's Death

Background: If only we knew the day of our death, perhaps we could live in anticipation of it. Since we can never know when we will die—only that we will indeed die—the rabbis have taught us to repent on the day of our death and live each day as if it were our last. This story focuses on King David's attempt to discover the day of his death.

King David said to the Holy Blessed One, "Master of the Universe, let me know when I will die!" God said to David, "It is My own decree that no human beings will be told their day of death." So David asked, "Then what will be the measure of my days?" To this, God answered, "It is My own decree that no humans should be told the measure of their days." [David continued,] "Let me know when I will die!" So God responded, "You will die on Shabbat." David pleaded, "Let me die on the first day of the week." But God responded, "On that day, your son Solomon's rule will begin. One's rule must not impinge on the other's rule, not even by a hair's breadth." God quoted the psalms [that are attributed to David]: "'A day in Your courts is better than a thousand elsewhere' [84:11]. It is better for Me that you sit and study Torah on one day than to receive a thousand burnt sacrifices that your son Solomon will offer up before Me on the altar."

From that point on, David sat and studied throughout the day every *Shabbat*. On the day on which he was to die, the Angel of Death came to David, but the angel was unable to touch David because he never ceased studying. The angel thought to himself, "What shall I do to him?" David had a garden behind his home. The angel went to the garden and violently shook the trees. When David rose from his study in order to investigate the noise, as he went down the stairs, a step broke under his feet. He fell silent and his soul departed.

Babylonian Talmud, *Shabbat* 30a-b

The Sulking Angel of Death

Background: Some say that we should have sympathy for the Angel of Death since she is just doing her job, fulfilling her responsibility to the world. And that is when she is happiest.

There were two Ethiopians, Elihoreph and Ahijah, the sons of Shisha (1 Kings 4:3), who served Solomon as scribes. One day, Solomon saw that the Angel of Death was sulking. Solomon said to the angel, "Why are you sulking?" The angel responded, "Because I was supposed to take these two Ethiopians who are sitting here." As a result, Solomon delivered them to the demons in Luz [in order to save their lives. The Angel of Death has no power there]. But as soon as they approached Luz, they died. The next day Solomon saw the Angel of Death, who was very happy. Solomon said to the angel, "Why are you so happy?" The Angel of Death's response was "Because you sent them to a place where I was required to take their lives." Spontaneously, Solomon remarked, "The feet of humans vouch for them; they take a person where that person is supposed to be."

Babylonian Talmud, *Sukkah* 53a

Tzedakah *or Death?*

Background: The giving of *tzedakah* is one of the many *mitzvot* that are said to ward off the Angel of Death. In this story, we have an example of how a person is kept alive in order to continue his good works in the world.

The sages tell a story about Benjamin the righteous, who was in charge of the *tzedakah* box. One day, in the years of drought, a woman came to him and said, "Rabbi, provide for me." Benjamin said to her, "By God, there is nothing left in the *tzedakah* box." But the woman continued, "If you do not provide for me, a woman and her seven children will die." So he took from his own [funds] and gave her money.

Only a few days later, Benjamin fell ill and was close to death. The ministering angels came to the Holy Blessed One and spoke [on Benjamin's behalf]: "Master of the Universe, You have said that 'if one saves a single life, it is as if that individual had saved the entire world.' Benjamin the righteous kept alive a woman and her seven children. Should he die in his early years [as a result of his charity]?" Instantly, his sentence of death was torn up and twenty-two more years were added to his life.

Babylonian Talmud, *Bava Batra* 11a

The End of Life

Background: Old age is considered by many the anteroom for death. In this story, a woman tells Rabbi Yose that she would rather die than continue life as she has come to know it in her old age.

Once a woman became old and went to Rabbi Yose ben Halafta and said to him, "Rabbi, I have become too old. My life is ghastly. I can taste neither food nor drink. All I want to do is pass from this world." The rabbi said to the woman, "What *mitzvah* do you do every day?" The woman replied, "Even if I am doing something that I like, I always leave it in order to go to the synagogue, every day, early in the morning." So the rabbi responded, "Do not go to the synagogue for three days in a row." She followed his advice, and on the third day she died.

Yalkut Shimoni 771

How We Die

Background: Perhaps what makes death so forbidding is that we do not know how we will die. That's part of the powerful images described in the *Unataneh Tokef* prayer recited on the High Holidays. This story tells us that our deeds determine how we will die.

How does a person die? Angels come to the person. One represents the ministering angels, one represents the Angel of Death, one is a scribe, and one represents the individual who is about to die. This last angel says to the person, "Get up. Your time has come." But the individual responds, "My end has not yet arrived."

Instantly, the person opens up his or her eyes and sees an angel whose size stretches from one end of the world to the other. From the soles of its feet to the top of its head, it is full of eyes. Its garment is made of fire. It is totally afire. A knife is in its hand, and a drop of gall hangs from the end of the knife. From that drop, which becomes putrid, the individual dies and the face of the individual turns green. But one cannot die until the individual sees the Holy Blessed One, for Scripture says, "For humans shall not see Me and live" (Exodus 33:20). In life, individuals cannot see God, but they can see God in death. At that point, one testifies about oneself, telling God everything one did in this world. Then the Holy Blessed One makes a sign. If the individual was pious, the individual delivers the soul to its owner, namely, God. If the person was totally wicked, the individual stiffens the neck and strengthens the *yetzer hara* (the evil inclination).

Massechet Chibbat Hakever, Bet Hamidrash 1:150

The Beating of Graves

Background: Disrespect for the dead is a serious offense in Judaism. It is believed that those who disrespect the dead—through the desecration of graves—will be punished for it. In this story, "the beating of graves to disturb the spirits" is described.

Rabbi Eliezer's students asked him, "What is the rule about the beating of the grave?" The rabbi told them, "When a person leaves this world, the Angel of Death comes and sits on the grave and beats it with its hand and says, 'Get up. Tell me your name.' So the dead person responds, 'It is revealed and well known before the One who said and the world came to be that I do not know my name.' As a result, the angel causes spirit and soul to enter the body of the dead person, making the person stand in judgment, finding that person guilty."

Rabbi Yehoshua ben Levi said, "A kind of chain is in the hand of the angel. Half of the chain is made of fire and half of it is made of iron. The angel strikes the individual once and the limbs fall off. A second time and the bones fall apart. So the ministering angels come and gather them, making them stand up. So the angel strikes a third time and asks an accounting of the individual, and punishes the person according to what he or she deserves. On the third day the individual is punished with beatings. The angel beats the eyes because he did not see and speak. The angel beats the ears because she did not hear and speak, and the lips, because he uttered obscene words with his lips, and the tongue because she bore false witness, and the feet because they made him hurry to transgress."

Massechet Chibbat Hakever, Bet Hamidrash 1:151

The Angel of Birth Becomes the Angel of Death

Background: Perhaps it is because death is considered part of life that there are stories—like this one—that suggest that the angel that accompanies the individual into this world at birth is the same one who accompanies the individual out of this world at death.

When a person's turn to die comes, the same angel that assisted at her birth comes and says to her, "Do you recognize me?" The person answers, "Yes," and continues, "why did you come for me today of all days?" So the angel responds, "In order to take you away from this world, for your time to depart has arrived." Instantly the person begins to cry, and her voice is heard from one end of the earth to the other. No creature recognizes her voice except for the rooster. So the person says to the angel, "You removed me from two worlds and placed me in this world. Why then do you want to take me out of this world?" The angel answers, "Did I not tell you that you were created against your will, born against your will, and will have to give an accounting before the Holy Blessed One against your will?"

Tanchuma, *Pekudei* 3

The Inheritance

Background: This story is about a man who dies while his son is many miles away. Thus, the man's servant assumes his wealth by pretending to be the son of the deceased. But he squanders the wealth and mistreats his former fellow servants. When the son returns home, he has to fight for his rightful inheritance. It seems we have to stand up for what is rightfully ours.

There was once a very rich man who lived at the time of King David. While he had many servants and much property, he only had one son, for whom he bought many things. Once, the son traveled on a ship to Africa, where he stayed for many years. During his time in Africa, the rich father died; he had left all of his worldly belongings under the supervision of one of his employees. Following the man's death, the one employee oppressed the other members of the household staff until they ran away. Thus, the one employee was left alone with all of the dead man's money and possessions. And he was happy. Or so he thought.

Eventually, the man's son returned from Africa and learned for the first time that his father had died during his long absence. Just when he was about to enter his family home, the remaining servant came out the door and pushed him away, saying, "Get out of here, you worthless bum!" In response, the son took a stick and hit the servant over the head. "You have taken my father's possessions and mine!" A fight ensued, and nobody tried to break it up. Eventually, the son fled and went directly to the king, asking for his guidance. "O king, may you live forever, this man has taken my father's possessions and taken over my home, telling me that I am not my father's son and not the heir to his fortune." "Have you any witnesses?" replied the king. "No," came the response. So the king summoned the former servant and asked of him the same question: "Have you any witnesses?" "No," came the same reply. "Then go in peace. You do not have to return anything."

When the old man's son overheard this conversation, he wept bitterly and sought out the king, rehearsing his tale of woe over and over again. Finally, the king lost his patience and rebuked him and said, "What can I do? If you have witnesses who can substantiate your claim, then I will force the servant to return your possessions to you. If you cannot do so and you continue to bother me, then I will have you punished."

The king's own son Solomon overheard his father's rebuke and motioned the young man to come to him, offering this advice: "Go to my father once again. If he rebukes you, tell him to give me the case to decide." The man followed Solomon's advice and the case indeed was given over to him to decide.

Solomon queried the son, "Do you know where your father is buried?" "No," came the response. Then Solomon asked the servant, who was pretending to be the real son, "Do you know where your father is buried?" "Yes," came the response.

So Solomon told the servant to go to his father's grave. "Cut off his arm and bring it to me." And the servant did as he was told. Then Solomon instructed both men to draw blood and let their blood flow into a container. Solomon said to the servant, "Dip the bone of your father into your blood." He did so, but the bone did not absorb the color of the blood. Yet when the son did the same thing, the bone became the color of the blood. And Solomon proclaimed to the people, "See, this blood came from this bone." The people of Israel were astonished at what Solomon had done. The money was given back to the son and the servant was ordered to serve the young man. That's why the Bible says, "Solomon was wiser than all humankind" (1 Kings 5:11).

Various traditional sources

Akiba's Death (1)

Background: Akiba joined his colleagues in a frightful death at the hands of the Romans, but even at his death he was able to fulfill the *mitzvot*, one of which he had to wait until his death to be able to fulfill.

Akiba was already forty years old when he came to learn Torah. His thirst for Torah could not be quenched even by the Romans, who forbade the study of Torah, declaring that whoever was caught studying or teaching Torah would be put to death. Unafraid, Akiba continued to teach his students in public.

But eventually he was caught. When he was taken out to be executed, Akiba was ready to recite the *Shema*. The Romans planned a torturous death for him, combing the flesh from his body with combs of iron, shredding his flesh until he died. But Akiba did not care about the pain. His disciples wondered how their teacher could endure such pain and still concentrate on holy things. Even at the end of his life, Akiba taught them: "All my life I was distressed when I declared my love for God *bechol nafshecha*. I am supposed to declare my love with all my soul, which means even if God takes away your life from you. I always wondered if I would be able to actually fulfill this *mitzvah*. And now, I finally have the opportunity to do so. How can I do anything else?" And putting what strength he had left in his body, he passionately uttered the word *echad*, and his soul returned to the Creator with the purity with which it had been given him.

Babylonian Talmud, *Berachot* 61b

Akiba's Death (2)

Background: This story from the Midrash emphasizes the important Jewish value of honoring the dead. Rabbi Akiba dies in prison and his body is laid to rest in a cave in preparation for the World to Come.

While Rabbi Akiba was in prison, the holiday of Yom Kippur arrived. Akiba's servant and disciple, Rabbi Joshua, went home.

Suddenly, the Prophet Elijah, always remembered for his good deeds, appeared at the doorstep of Rabbi Joshua. "*Shalom*," Elijah said to Rabbi Joshua. "Peace be unto you," Rabbi Joshua answered.

Thereupon Elijah said, "Do you need anything?"

"Who are you?" queried Rabbi Joshua, obviously not recognizing him.

Elijah answered, "I am a priest and I came to tell you that Rabbi Akiba has just died in prison." Immediately, both hurried to the prison and found the prison door open. The head warden and all of the prisoners were asleep. Elijah and Rabbi Joshua laid out Rabbi Akiba's corpse on a bier and were about to leave when Elijah decided to hoist the bier on his own shoulders. Seeing this, Rabbi Joshua said, "Did you not tell me that you were a priest, and is not a priest forbidden to defile himself by coming into contact with the dead?"

Elijah answered, "Enough, Rabbi Joshua. God forbid that disciples of the wise or even their disciples should convey uncleanliness."

So that night the two carried Rabbi Akiba's body until they reached Antipatris of Caesarea. After arriving, they went up three steps, down three steps, and a cave opened up before them! In it they saw a seat, a footstool, a table, and a lamp. They laid down the bier of Rabbi Akiba and left.

Moments later, the cave closed and the light in the lamp was lit. Seeing this, Elijah burst forth in blessing: "Blessed are you, the righteous ones who labor in Torah! Blessed are you who fear God. In the time to come, a place in the Garden of Eden is reserved for you. Blessed are you, Rabbi Akiba, that at the time of your death a transient lodging was made available to you."

Proverbs Rabbah 9

The Day of Death

Background: The teaching "Repent one day before your death" encourages us to take a hard look at our life every day, since we never know when it will be our last. This story explores that well-known teaching.

Rabbi Eliezer taught his students, "Repent one day before you die." As would be expected, of course, his students queried their teacher, "But how can a person know when he or she is about to die so that a person might repent the day before?" Rabbi Eliezer responded, "That's the point. Since a person may never know the day of death, one should repent every day, since tomorrow may indeed be one's final day." Ecclesiastes had said the same thing when he said, "Your clothing should be white every day" (Ecclesiastes 9:8).

In order to emphasize this teaching, Rabbi Yochanan ben Zakkai offered the following parable: A king once invited his entire palace household to a feast. "Get prepared for the banquet, but I am not going to tell you when it is going to take place." Said a foolish servant, "This banquet will probably not be held for a long time. We can go about our daily routines. As soon as we see that preparations are being made for the party, we can change our clothing and get ready."

The more insightful servants disagreed. "The king's palace lacks nothing. He can arrange a banquet in quite a short time. If we do not get ready now, we will be caught unprepared." And so they put on their finery in anticipation of the banquet.

To everyone's surprise, the king suddenly made an announcement: "All of my servants are requested to come to the banquet." The wiser servants entered the banquet hall, having been prepared for the announcement to come. They were well groomed and well dressed. However, in an effort not to be late—thinking that tardiness might offend the king—the foolish servants rushed into the banquet without taking the time to wash themselves or change their clothing. To the well groomed, the king said, "You understood and you shall be rewarded." To the others, he said, "Fools. Did I not warn you that I could call you at a moment's notice? You do not deserve to share in the bounty of my palace."

Feeling foolish and remorseful, these servants humbly asked the king, "What can we do?" The king responded, "Stand by and watch your friends enjoying the banquet. The pain you experience in watching them is what you deserve."

After Rabbi Yochanan had told this story, he sought to clarify its message. "The righteous are the clever ones in this story. Knowing that God could call them at any moment, they sought to prepare themselves each day by repenting and doing good deeds. When they die, their souls will go straight to heaven. They will be admitted to *Gan Eden*, the banquet hall, in order to enjoy the presence of the *Shechinah*. The foolish ones, on the other hand, are the wicked who occupy their place on earth. It is their *yetzer hara*, their evil inclination, that induces them to sin. They think they can go about doing just as they please—with no consequences. When the time comes for their final accounting, they reach heaven in filthy clothing; their souls are stained with sin. They are punished by watching the *tzadikim* basking in the reflective glory of God."

Babylonian Talmud, *Shabbat* 153a

A Ticket to the World to Come

Background: This midrashic story explains the importance of the *mitzvah* of caring for the aged and the reward of the World to Come that results from its performance.

Once Rabbi Joshua ben Ilem dreamed that his neighbor in Paradise would be Nanas, the meat dealer. He decided to visit him in order to ascertain what good deeds he was performing to deserve such an important place in Paradise. The dealer said, "I don't really know, but I do have an aged father and mother who are quite helpless. Every day I give them food and drink and I wash them too."

The rabbi answered, "I will be happy to have you as my neighbor in Paradise."

Seder Hadorot

A Child's Prayer

Background: This chasidic story focuses on the power of true prayer and its ability to get the attention of God's mercy.

Once Rabbi Eliezer and his students were traveling on the road toward the city of Peki'in. Nearing the city, they heard a cry: "Rabbi Yose has died!"

Rabbi Eliezer clasped his hands in anguish and cried, "This wonderful fruit has been taken from us!" Turning to his students, he said, "Come, let us visit the home of this great man and mourn him."

Upon entering Rabbi Yose's home, they found his young son kneeling before his father's casket and crying.

"O God," he cried, "why did You take my father away? In Your Torah it states: If a person finds a nest of birds, you shall send away the mother bird and keep the baby birds. O God, You know that my sister and I have no mother. Our father was to us like a mother. Now why did You take our father, who is like our mother, and send us away? The Torah states that You should send the mother away and take the babies—us. What benefit can You derive from leaving two little orphans alone in the world?"

When Rabbi Eliezer and his students heard this plea, they all began to cry. It was then that Rabbi Eliezer prayed to God.

Suddenly, a fire descended from heaven and surrounded the little boy and his father's casket. A heavenly voice rang out: "You are lucky, Rabbi Yose, that you have such an intelligent son. His tears and prayers reached Me.

Turning to the grieving son, God continued, "I, God, have decreed that your father shall come back to life. He will live another twenty-two years, so that you will be able to be instructed in Torah."

The heavenly fire lifted, and Rabbi Yose suddenly opened his eyes. "Praised be God that we were worthy enough to see the resurrection of the dead," cried Rabbi Eliezer.

They approached the coffin and saw that the little boy had fainted. After helping Rabbi Yose to arise, they took the boy and bathed his face, thus reviving him. He then hugged his father and could not stop crying tears of joy.

"Lucky you are, Rabbi Yose, that you have such a wonderful son whose prayers penetrated the heavens."

"Listen to me, my friends," said Rabbi Yose. "In heaven they counted all the tears of my son. He shed three hundred seventy tears, which flew directly to the heavenly court. The heavens trembled and Satan and his accusers became mute. Then when my son quoted the sentence in the Torah about the mother bird, all the angels began to shake and the plea came directly to God, who commanded that my soul be returned."

Rabbi Eliezer and his disciples remained in the home of Rabbi Yose for thirty days, celebrating his return with parties and praises of *Hallel*.

Chasidic story

My Neighbor in Paradise

Background: This chasidic story expresses the importance and efficacy of true and sincere prayer that is from the heart.

Once, the Baal Shem Tov was curious to know who would be his neighbor in Paradise. When he learned that it would be a certain shepherd, he was anxious to know what made him worthy of reaching Paradise. Questioning the shepherd, the Baal Shem Tov soon learned that he could neither read nor write. It was then that the Baal Shem Tov decided that the shepherd must be a man of extreme piety. Upon reaching his decision, he decided to evaluate his actions on the day of Yom Kippur.

Yom Kippur arrived, and hiding behind a tree, the Baal Shem Tov observed the shepherd with great intensity. The shepherd stayed with his flock as usual. However, when the sheep gathered to eat of the vegetation, the shepherd began to pray, "O God, I know that today is Yom Kippur, a most holy day, when Jews fast and pray. However, I do not know how to pray, because my parents died when I was very young and they were unable to teach me. So how can I pray to You? I know how to dance. May it be Your will that my dancing will be regarded as prayer."

The shepherd began to dance until he almost collapsed from exhaustion. Upon his recovery he again prayed, "O God, I love You with all my heart and soul. I know how to play a flute, so I will play a melody on it as my prayer." He then proceeded to play.

Later he said, "O God, how can I serve You? In an entire year I earn only two gold coins. With one I keep

my body and soul together, and the other I give to You."
He took the gold coin and tossed it upward toward heaven.
The Baal Shem Tov noticed that a hand of fire appeared
from heaven to take the coin. It was then that the Baal Shem
Tov realized how priceless was the simple piety of the
shepherd.

Chasidic story

The Nut of the
Spinal Column

Background: In this story from the *Midrash* we learn from
which part of the body a person will "sprout" forth in the
World to Come.

Hadrian, may his bones be crushed, once asked Rabbi
Joshua ben Chananiah, "From which part of the body will
the Holy Blessed One, in the Time to Come, cause humans
to sprout forth?"

Rabbi Joshua answered, "From the nut of the spinal
column." He then asked him, "How can you convince me?"
Whereupon Rabbi Joshua brought one before him. He put
water on it, and it was not dissolved. He let it pass through
millstones, but it was not ground. He put it in fire, but it
did not burn! He put it on an anvil and began beating it
with a hammer, but the anvil was flattened and the hammer split; all this had no effect.

Leviticus Rabbah 18:1

Death Omens

Background: This talmudic story provides insight into the different ways people die and the symbolism behind their deaths.

If a person dies smiling, it is a good omen. If a person dies crying, it is a bad omen. If a person's face is turned upward, it is a good omen. If it is turned downward, it is a bad omen. If one faces the people around him, it is a good omen. If she faces the wall, it is a bad omen. If a person's face is greenish, it is a bad omen. If a person's face is bright and ruddy, that is a good omen. If a person dies on the eve of *Shabbat*, it is a good omen. If a person dies when *Shabbat* ends, that is a bad omen. If a person dies at the outgoing of the Day of Atonement, it is a good omen. If a person dies of a disease of the bowels, it is a good omen, because most of the righteous die of such a disease.

Babylonian Talmud, *Ketubot* 103a

The True Friend

Background: This short talmudic story is an attempt to show that a person's deeds are the most important part of any person's life. Good deeds will be remembered forever and pave a path to eternity for that person.

A person had three friends. One friend she loved a great deal, a second she also loved, but the third she regarded with much less affection. One day the woman lost everything she owned. The king commanded her to appear before him immediately. The woman was very frightened, wondering why the king would want to speak to her. In fear, she called upon each of her three friends to escort her to the king.

First, she turned to her dearest friend, and was extremely disappointed when this friend said it would be impossible to go with her to visit the king.

She then turned to her second friend. "Will you go with me to the king?" This friend said, "I can go with you only up to the gates of the palace, but that is as far as I can go."

Extremely dejected, the woman then turned to her third friend, the one to whom she had shown the most disregard. This friend said with assurance, "I will accompany you, but first I will go directly to the palace myself and plead for you with the king."

The first friend in the parable reflects a person's wealth, which cannot accompany you to the grave, as it is written, "Riches profit not in the day of reckoning."

The second friend represents a person's relatives, who can only follow you to the grave site, as it is written, "No person can redeem his brother [or sister] from death."

The third and last friend in the story portrays the good deeds of a person's life. These never desert you and even precede you to plead your cause before the Sovereign of all Sovereigns, as it is written, "And your righteousness shall go before you."

Adapted from *Pirke de Rabbi Eliezer*

The Rose Talked Back

Background: This story has as its theme a reminder that it may not be the length of life that a living thing enjoys that counts in this world. Rather, real worth is measured in the amount of joy given to another person even through a brief life.

The man sweeping the synagogue paused for a moment. He looked at the flowers lying about in disorder. "What waste!" he said to himself. Those roses had adorned the pulpit at a wedding an hour before. Now all was over and they were waiting to be discarded.

The attendant leaning on his sweeper was lost in thought when suddenly he heard a strange sound. One of the roses replied to him.

"Do you call this a waste?" the flower protested. "What is life anyway, yours or mine, but a means of service? My mission was to create some fragrance and beauty, and as I have fulfilled it, my life has not been wasted. What greater privilege is there than to adorn a bride's way to her beloved; what greater privilege than to help glorify the moment when a bride and groom seal their faith in each other by entering the covenant of marriage?"

The little flower paused for a moment to watch the man's face and then continued her discourse.

"Roses are like people. They live in deeds, not in time. My glory was brief, only an hour, but you should have seen the joy in the bride's face. I like to believe that I had something to do with it by creating a suitable setting for the moment of her happiness. So don't grieve for me. My life has been worthwhile."

Having made her statement, the rose was once more silent. The attendant, startled from his reverie and a little wiser, pushed the sweeper again and continued with his work.

Ben Zion Bokser

The Impending Death of Rabbi Zusya

Background: While we often wish we were someone else or had that person's ability for a particular skill, this well-known story reminds us that we should try to make something out of our lives with whatever unique talents God gave us. If we can live our lives knowing we have done just that, then we really have nothing to fear at the end of our days.

When the students of Zusya approached their dying teacher, he whispered to them, "My students, I am very afraid!"

His students were shocked and responded, "Reb Zusya, did you not always teach us that we should have no fear of dying because God is our Parent and God is filled with kindness and compassion?"

"That's true," replied Zusya, "but that is not why I am so frightened. I am not afraid that when I stand before the Throne of Judgment God will say to me, 'Zusya, why were you not a Moses?' because I am not Moses. And I am not afraid that God will say to me, 'Why were you not an Isaiah?' because I am not an Isaiah. But, my dear students, I am afraid that when God asks me, 'Zusya, why were you not Zusya? Why didn't you live up to the best that Zusya could have been?' I am afraid, for what shall I answer?"

Chasidic story

The Death of Absalom

Background: This biblical narrative reminds us that we ought not to become overly melancholy when death strikes. We should not grieve too much. Instead, what is important is the memory of those whom we love who have died and to continue living life in their memory—through the examples they have set before us.

Now it happened that the child did die. And the servants of King David were afraid to tell him that the child was dead, for they reasoned, "While his child was still alive, he did not listen to us when we spoke to him. How, then, can we now tell him that the child is dead? If we do, he may do himself harm."

When King David noticed that his servants were whispering to each other, he realized right then that the child was dead. Then King David asked his servants, "Is the child dead?" They answered, "He is dead."

King David arose from the ground and washed and changed his clothes, went to the House of God, and there he prayed. Then he went to his own home and they set food before him and he ate. His servants asked him, "What is this that you have done?" And King David replied, "While the child was still alive, I fasted and wept, for I said, 'Who knows whether God will be gracious to me, that the child may live?' But now he is dead, why should I not eat? Can I bring him back? I shall go to him, but he will not return to me."

2 Samuel, chapter 12

The Queen's Diamond

Background: When death comes, pain is deep. However, our challenge is to use the "scratches" to etch a portrait of beauty through the memory of the deceased.

Once upon a time a queen owned a very large and beautiful diamond. The queen was very proud of her gem, for there was nothing else like it in the entire world. One day, the gem was accidentally dropped and it sustained a very deep scratch. The queen wanted to repair it and called together all of the best diamond cutters and merchants in the land, offering them a large reward for removing the imperfection. But not one of them could fix the diamond, and the queen was extremely distressed.

After some time, a gifted craftsperson came to the queen and promised to make the rare diamond even more beautiful than it had been before it was scratched. The queen was impressed and gave the gem to the craftsperson.

The craftsperson kept his word, and with superb artistry, he engraved a lovely rosebud around the imperfection, using the scratch to make the stem. The queen was very happy, and the craftsperson was greatly rewarded for his efforts.

Adapted from a story told by the Dubner Maggid

Questions about Death and the World to Come

Background: This talmudic story relates the questions that are asked of the deceased when he or she reaches the gates of the World to Come.

Rava once said, "When a person is brought to judgment in the World to Come, these questions will be asked: Did you conduct your affairs with integrity? Did you set aside fixed times for study? Did you occupy yourself with raising a family? Did you hope for Israel's redemption and for peace in the world? Did you search for wisdom? Did you acquire understanding?

"If the answer to all of these questions is yes, but the person did not treasure reverence for God, all the learning and the fulfillment of the *mitzvot* were of little value."

Babylonian Talmud, *Shabbat* 31a

The Deathbed of Akavya ben Mahalel

Background: This talmudic story describes the importance of a person's good deeds and how they affect people even after death.

When Akavya ben Mahalel was on his deathbed, his son requested, "Father, commend me to your colleagues."

Akavya replied, "I will not commend you."

His son asked, "Have you found some fault with me?"

His father answered, "No. But your own good deeds will bring you near to them without any commendation, and your own bad deeds will remove you far from them despite any commendation."

Jerusalem Talmud, *Eduyot* 5:7

The Day of Judgment: Body and Soul

Background: This talmudic story describes the close relationship between body and soul and their shared responsibility for all of the deeds of a person.

A Roman emperor once said to Judah the Prince, "On the Day of Judgment, the soul and body will each plead excuses for sins they committed. The body will say, 'It was not me. Rather, it was the soul that sinned. For without a soul, I am lifeless as a stone.' But the soul will say, 'How could I have sinned? Surely the body is responsible.'"

Rabbi Judah the Prince replied with a parable: A king once had a beautiful garden in which fruit trees grew. He hired two men, one blind and one lame, to guard the fruit-tree garden. One day, the lame man said to the blind one, "There is delicious fruit on these trees."

The blind man then suggested, "Climb on my shoulder and you can pick some so that we can enjoy it together."

The king, missing the fruit, summoned the two men together for punishment.

"How could I have taken the fruit?" asked the lame man. "I can't even walk."

"Could I have stolen the fruit?" asked the blind man. "I cannot see."

The very wise king then had the lame man placed on the shoulders of the blind man, and then he condemned them together as one.

Similarly, the Divine Judge of the Universe will sentence jointly the body along with the soul.

Various traditional sources

The Ripe Fig

Background: Some people die at a young age. This story from the *midrash* gives one of several rationales for early death, none of which is acceptable to most people.

In hot weather, a particular rabbi delivered his lecture to his students under the shade of a fig tree. They noticed that every morning the owner of the tree would pick the figs that had ripened on the tree. "Maybe he is afraid we will pick his fruit," the students thought, and they moved to another place.

The owner begged them to return. Since he believed that the students had moved because his presence annoyed them, he resolved not to pick the fruit. In the evening, the students saw the figs dropping from the tree, spoiled by the heat of the searing sun. The students then appreciated why it was necessary for the owner always to pick the figs in the morning.

The rabbi said, "The owner of the figs knows when his fruit should be picked, so that it will not spoil. So too God knows when to summon God's righteous children before they are spoiled. This is the reason good and gracious people are sometimes called by God when they are still young."

Song of Songs Rabbah 6:2

The Time of Judgment

Background: This tale from the *midrash* reminds us that righteous people enter the gates of Heaven when they die. They are given special honor because of all the kind and righteous deeds they performed in the land of the living.

At the time of judgment, everyone will be asked, "What was your occupation?" If the person answers, "I used to feed the hungry," they will say to him, "This is God's gate. You who fed the hungry may enter."

If at the time of judgment the person answers, "I used to give water to those who were thirsty," they will say to her, "This is God's gate. You who gave water to those who were thirsty may enter."

If at the time of judgment the person answers, " I used to clothe the naked," they will say to him, "This is God's gate. You who clothed the naked may enter." Similarly, those who raised orphans and who performed the *mitzvah* of *tzedakah* and acts of caring and loving-kindness will be allowed to enter.

Psalms Rabbah 118

A Man in Sepphoris

Background: God is able to do wonders in the World to Come, so claims this story.

Once upon a time there was a man in Sepphoris whose son had died. A heretic sat by his side. Rabbi Jose ben Halafta came to visit him. The heretic saw that he was smiling and said, "Rabbi, why are you smiling?"

The rabbi replied, "I trust God and believe that the man will see his son again in the World to Come."

The heretic then said, "Is not his sorrow enough for the man that you should come and sadden him even more? Can broken shards be made to fit together again? Is it not written, 'You shall break them in pieces like a potter's vessel?'"

The rabbi replied, "Earthen vessels are made by water and perfected by fire. Vessels of glass are both made by fire and perfected by fire. Earthen ones, if broken, cannot be repaired, but glass ones, if broken, can be repaired."

The heretic asked, "Why?"

The rabbi replied, "Because glass vessels are made by blowing. If the glass vessel that is made by the blowing of a mortal person can be repaired, how much more the being who is made by the blowing of God."

Genesis Rabbah 14:7

The Last Words

Background: This talmudic story reflects the interest of the rabbis in deeds of righteousness prior to a person's death.

When Mar Ukba was very close to death, he asked that his record of charities be tallied and reported. It was found that Mar Ukba had distributed seven thousand dinars. When he learned of this, he sighed and said, "The way before me is very long, and the provision I have prepared for myself is very small." And he ordered that one half of all of his possessions be given to charity.

It was asked, How was he able to do so? Did not Rabbi Elai say that the Great Sanhedrin Court of Law at Usha adopted a resolution that no person could give more than one-fifth of his property to charity at one time?

The answer is this: This resolution applied to one who was in good and sound health, lest the person become impoverished. It did not apply, however, in the case of Mar Ukba, a man so near to death.

Babylonian Talmud, *Ketubot* 67b

Last Respects

Background: This story from the Talmud emphasizes the honor shown to Rabbi Akiba at the funeral of his two children.

It happened that two young children of Rabbi Akiba died. Numerous people came to pay last respects to them. Rabbi Akiba stood on a high stool and cried out, "O brothers and sisters of Israel. Listen to me. Even if my sons had been old enough to be bridegrooms, I would feel consoled by the great honor you are showing me. But have you come for the sake of Akiba? No, for there are many whose names are Akiba. You have said to yourself, 'The Torah of God is in your heart' [Psalm 37:31]. You came to honor the Torah and your reward is great. Go back to your homes in peace."

Babylonian Talmud, *Mo'ed Katan* 21b

A Time to Be Born, a Time to Die

Background: This story was written as a commentary on the verse from Ecclesiastes (7:1) "A good name is better than fragrant oil, and the day of death better than the day of birth."

When a person is born, everyone is happy and celebrates. But when a person dies, everyone cries. It really should not be this way. For when a person is born, there should be no rejoicing because no one knows what will happen to the person or in which direction the person will go. The person could go the way of the righteous, or the person could be evil and go the way of all of the wicked.

When a person dies, there is cause to rejoice if the person departs with a good name and leaves the world in peace.

To what can this be likened? A parable can be drawn to two ships that sailed on a great sea, one leaving the harbor and the other entering it. Everybody cheered the ship that sailed out of the harbor, but nobody rejoiced over the ship that entered.

A shrewd person was there, and he said, "My view is the exact opposite of yours. There is no reason to rejoice over the ship that is leaving the harbor because no one knows what will be its fate or what seas and terrible storms it might encounter. But everybody should cheer the ship that is entering the harbor because it left the seas peacefully and returned to the harbor safely."

And that is what Solomon meant when he said, "And the day of death is better than the day of one's birth."

Ecclesiastes Rabbah 7:4

The Comfort of Rabbi Yochanan ben Zakkai

Background: This talmudic story emphasizes the important religious obligation to comfort the mourner.

When Rabbi Yochanan ben Zakkai's son died, all of his disciples came to comfort him. Rabbi Elazar ben Arach sat down in front of him and said, "I am going to tell you a parable. To what can your situation be compared? It is like a person to whom the king has given something to be taken care of. Every day the person would weep and say, "Woe is me. When shall I be free of this thing and once again be at peace?"

So too it is with you, my teacher. You had a son who studied all of the Torah, and the *Mishnah*, and the legal and nonlegal sections, and he left the world with a clean slate and without sin. Now that you have returned what was entrusted to you, it is appropriate for you to be comforted."

Rabbi Yochanan then said to him, "Elazar, my son, you have comforted me the way people ought to give comfort."

Avot de Rabbi Natan, chapter 14

The Death of Aaron

Background: Preparation for death can be made by some for whom death is imminent. This story attempts to explain Aaron's preparation for death and his death.

When Aaron was approaching the time of his death, God said to his brother Moses, "Go to your brother and tell him about his impending death."

The very next morning Moses arose and went to Aaron's tent. Aaron asked, "Why have you come to my tent so early in the morning?"

Moses replied, "I am worried about a certain section of the Torah that I was thinking about all night long, so I came to you."

Aaron then asked, "Where is the problem found?"

Moses answered, "I believe it is somewhere in the Book of Genesis."

They brought out the Torah scroll and began to read. At each part of the creation story, Moses said, "God made it beautiful." But when they reached the story of the creation of Adam, Moses said, "What can be said about Adam, who brought death to the world? Look, Aaron, I have prevailed over angels and you have stopped the plague of death, but even so our own end will be death. How many more years do you think we have?"

Aaron answered, "Very few."

Moses continued to get closer and closer to the subject of death until he referred to the surety of his own death. Soon Aaron began to feel that he would soon die and asked his brother Moses, "Did you come here to tell me about my own death?"

"Yes," answered Moses.

Soon thereafter Moses asked his brother, "Are you reconciled to the idea that you will die?"

Aaron responded, "Yes."

Then Moses said, "Let's together climb up to Mount Hor."

So Moses, Aaron, and Aaron's son Eleazar went up the mountain as all the people watched, thinking that they had been called to receive God's instructions. Had they known the true purpose of the journey, they probably would have stopped them and begged mercy for Aaron.

Reaching the top of Mount Hor, they found a cave, and on entering it they saw a lit lamp and a bed. Everything had been prepared by God! Moses was told to remove Aaron's priestly clothes. As he took off each garment, his son Eleazar put it on—just as darkness began to surround Aaron.

Then Moses spoke. "Aaron, when our sister Miriam died, you and I attended to her and buried her. At your death, you are attended to by Eleazar and me. But when I die, who will attend my burial?"

God then answered, "I promise that I will attend to you."

Moses then continued and said, "Brother Aaron, lie down on this couch and stretch out your hands. Close your eyes and your lips."

Aaron followed these instructions. Then God's Presence descended and touched Aaron and his soul left him. Moses and Eleazar kissed Aaron and the Cloud of Glory covered him.

God then told them, "Leave the cave."

Moses and Eleazar left, and the cave closed by itself. When Moses and Eleazar descended Mount Hor, all the people stood and watched. They looked for Aaron, the lover of peace. When they finally realized that only two were coming down from the mountain, their concern was aggravated by Satan, who incited them against Moses and Eleazar. The community divided itself into three factions.

One faction said, "Moses killed Aaron out of jealousy."

A second cried out, "Eleazar killed his father out of his desire to succeed him."

The third faction suggested that Aaron died a natural death.

When Moses and Eleazar finally reached the people, the people demanded to know what happened to Aaron. Moses said to them, "God has taken him to the World to Come."

"We do not believe you!" they retorted. "You must have had a disagreement and you killed Aaron for saying something that you didn't like."

The people became wild with anger and were about to stone Moses and Eleazar when God ordered the angels to open the cave and bring out Aaron's coffin, which was seen by all of the people as it stood suspended in the heavens, surrounded by singing angels. So we read in the Bible, "And all the people saw that Aaron was dead" (Numbers 20:29). And what were the angels singing? "He entered into peace, they rest in their beds each one that walks in his uprightness" (Isaiah 57:2).

Yalkut, *Chukkat* 764

Jacob's Death

Background: This story attempts to explain the timing of the death of Jacob, who had gathered his sons together in order to receive his blessing, as reflected in Genesis 49:1-33.

Jacob called his sons and said to them, "Assemble yourselves and I will tell you." Jacob wanted to reveal the future to his children, but the Divine Spirit left him at that very moment. In truth, it was because it would be wrong for them to know what the future held. But Jacob said, "Perhaps one of my children will turn out to be no good. After all, Abraham had Ishmael, and Isaac had Esau."

Upon hearing these words, his children proclaimed, "Hear O Israel, *Adonai* our God, *Adonai* is One. Just as there is only one God for you, so for us there is only One God."

Reassured, Jacob then proclaimed, "Praised be God's Name forever and ever."

Babylonian Talmud, *Pesachim* 56a; *Genesis Rabbah* 98:4

The Death of Moses (1)

Background: One of the most puzzling aspects of Moses' leadership was his inability to enter the Promised Land. One wonders why God chose Moses to lead the people from slavery only to have him die in the desert just before crossing the Jordan River. This story attempts to explain theologically why God punished Moses and would not allow him to enter into the Promised Land.

As Moses grew closer to his death, he began to pray to God for forgiveness for his sins. He wanted to be allowed to enter the Promised Land. Moses prayed, "O Sovereign of the Universe, You chose me in mercy to be Your servant. You have performed great miracles in Egypt. But now You say to me that I will die and my end will be like dust and worms."

God replied, "No person can escape death. Even Adam, who I made with My own hands, was doomed to die."

Moses responded, "O God, You gave only one command to the first person, and Adam disobeyed it."

God then responded, "I have heard enough. Speak to Me no longer."

But Moses continued to plead, "You forgive all Your creatures many sins with Your mercy and kindness. Cannot You overlook my one single sin?"

God replied, "I have made two vows. First, you will die before the Israelites enter the Promised Land. Second, Israel shall be forgiven and not be allowed to die. If I break My first vow, I must also cancel My second, and Israel will have to die."

To this Moses replied, "Rather shall I and a thousand like me die than a single soul in Israel."

Deuteronomy Rabbah 11:10

The Death of Moses (2)

Background: Since there is little biblical material that describes the death of Moses, much of what is written in the tradition concerning his death is taken from the midrash. Even the burial place of Moses is shrouded in secrecy. This tale is taken from the midrash on the Book of Proverbs (chapter 14). This legend takes advantage of the lack of knowledge about Moses' burial place by providing us with details that serve to describe our teacher in familiar human terms. We learn some interesting details about preparing for death both from the perspective of one who is dying and from those who survive Moses as future leaders of the Jewish community.

This account is based on Rabbi Simon's interpretation of the verse in Isaiah (58:8) "Your righteousness shall walk before you." Rabbi Simon says that this verse refers to the death of Moses, since it is written in the Book of Deuteronomy, "He comes as the head of the people, for he has performed the righteousness of God."

R abbi Abbahu said, "Come and let us see how difficult it was at the hour of Moses', our master's, departure from the world. For when God told him, 'Moses, your time has come to leave the world,' Moses began to cry and scream. He asked God, 'Master of the Universe, was it for nothing that I spent all of my strength working for my people? Now shall my finale be the grave, my end as dust? If You could see it my way, You would cause me suffering but not hand me over to the pangs of death.' Of this David spoke, 'God, afflict me with suffering, but do not let me die' [Psalm 118:18].

"God answered Moses, 'Moses, I have taken an oath that one's leadership may not overlap another's by even a hairbreadth. Thus far, you were leader of the Israelites; now it is time for Joshua to be their new leader.'

"With this Moses answered God, 'Lord of the Universe, in the past I was the master and Joshua was my student. Now, I'll be his disciple and he shall be my master. Just don't let me die!'

"God said, 'If you can do it, Moses, go right ahead.'

"Moses immediately went to Joshua's door, where he stood in service upon Joshua with his arms crossed and body bowed. Joshua did not truly realize that it was Moses standing in service upon him.

"As was their custom, the Israelites rose early to pay their respects at Moses' door, but on this day they did not find him. They asked, 'Where can Moses be?' and they were told, 'He rose early in the morning to pay his respects at Joshua's door.' So they went and found Joshua seated and Moses standing as a servant before him. They asked, 'Joshua, Joshua, what is this you have done? Moses your master stands in service upon you?'

"At that moment Joshua realized what was happening. Immediately he fell on his face before Moses and cried, 'Father, Master. You have raised me since I was a child, and you have taught me wisdom.'

"The sons of Aaron stood on Moses' right and Joshua on his left. They asked him, 'Moses, what have you done?' He replied, 'Leave me alone, for God has told me that I should do this for Joshua so I will not die.'"

Rabbi Shmuel bar Nachmani quoted Rabbi Yochanan, "At that moment all the Israelites sought to stone Joshua to death but for the pillar of cloud that interposed between them.

"They then said to Moses, 'Conclude the Torah for us!' But all of the traditions were forgotten by Moses and he did not know how to answer them.

"At this failure Moses fell to his face and said, 'O God, my death is better than my life' [Jonah 4:3].

"When God saw that Moses was ready to die, God eulogized him, 'It is written, "Who will stand up to Me for this nation of wicked, who will stand watch for Me on behalf of this nation of evildoers?" [Psalm 94:16]. Who will stand up to Me in the wars of My children when they sin before Me?'

"At that moment the angel Michael came and bowed before God and said, 'Sovereign of the Universe, Moses was Yours in life, so he is Yours in death.' God responded, 'I lament not for Moses but for Israel, for many was the time that they sinned and he stood and prayed and tempered My anger, as it is said, "God would have destroyed them but for Moses, God's chosen one, who stood in the breach and assuaged God's anger from its destroying fury"' [Psalm 106:23].

"The Israelites then came and said to Moses, 'The moment for your departure from this world has arrived.' He said to them, 'Israel, O my children, forgive me for all that I have troubled you.' They answered, 'Our Master, Moses, you are forgiven.' They then said to him, 'Moses, forgive us all that we have angered you.' He told them, 'My children, you are forgiven, you are forgiven.'

"They came and told him, 'But half a moment remains for you to depart this world.' He took his two hands and folded them upon his heart. Crying, he said, 'Surely my two hands, which received the Torah from the mouth of God, will now fall to the grave.'

"They came and said to him, 'The moment for your

departure from this world is ending.' At that moment Moses cried out mightily to God. He said, 'Master of both Worlds, if You take my soul in this world, will You return it to me in the Coming World?'

"God answered, 'By your life! Just as you were the head of them all in this world, so will you be the head of them all in the Future World,' as it is written, "He comes as the head of the people"' [Deuteronomy 33:21]. Why so? Because of the righteousness he performed for Israel, as it is said, 'He has done the righteousness of God, and His judgment is with Israel' [Deuteronomy 33:21]."

Rabbi Nehemiah explained, "What did he do? He taught them Torah, laws, and righteousness."

Proverbs Rabbah, chapter 14

The Rejection of Moses' Plea

Background: This story demonstrates Moses' persistence as he attempts to convince God to allow him to enter into the Promised Land.

Moses was about to die and made a last effort to obtain God's mercy. He said to God, "I have never seen the Promised Land and I want to go there to fulfill Your *mitzvot*. Forgive, I beg You, my sin, so that all who know You will call You Merciful One."

God answered, "Your sin will not be forgiven, so that all people shall know that I do not discriminate even in favor of a person like you, with whom I speak face-to-face."

Moses replied, "O God, if I cannot enter the Promised Land as the leader of the people, let me enter as the humblest of them all."

God answered, "I cannot grant you this wish either."

Then Moses pleaded, "O God, change me into a beast that eats grass and drinks water, but let me enter the Promised Land."

To this God replied, "I cannot grant you this request either."

Then Moses said, "If You cannot change me into an animal, then change me into a bird and let me enter the Promised Land."

"Enough," answered God. "My decision will not change!"

When Moses heard God's final decision he responded, "Rock of Ages, Your ways are just. But permit me to make one more request of You. Let the heavens be opened and the abyss be torn asunder so that Your people will see that You are the One and Only."

When Moses finished this request, the heavens immediately opened and the abyss was torn asunder. All the eyes of the Israelites were opened to experience the Presence of God. Then they all cried out together, "Hear, O Israel, *Adonai* is Our God, *Adonai* is One."

Various traditional sources

The Burial of Moses

Background: This story from the Talmud is a commentary on the verse from Deuteronomy (34:6) "And God buried him in a valley in the land of Moab, over against Beth-Peor." It is an attempt to establish God's reason for not clearly identifying the place of Moses' burial.

The wicked rulers of Rome once ordered a military party at Beth-Peor in an attempt to find the sepulcher of Moses. When they ascended on high ground, it appeared as if it were in the valley. However, when they stood in the valley, it appeared as if it were on high ground.

Rabbi Hama b. Haninah said, "Why was the burial place of Moses hidden from all people's knowledge? Because God knew that the time in the future would come when the Temple would be destroyed and Israel would be exiled from their land. If the Israelites knew where Moses was buried, they would be tempted to go to the sepulcher and cry and plead to Moses, saying, 'Moses, pray for us!' Moses would do so and the decree would be annulled, because the righteous are even more precious to God after their death than while they are alive."

Babylonian Talmud, *Sotah* 13a–b

The Chastisement of the Angel of Death

Background: This is another in a series of legends that deal with the impending death of Moses and the dispute over who, among the angels, will be charged to take his soul.

When God saw that Moses was ready to die, he said to the angel Gabriel, "Fetch for me the soul of Moses."

Gabriel replied, "O God, how can I take the soul out of a person who brought so many miracles?"

To which God replied, "Noah was a righteous person in My eyes, and he died. Abraham also did not escape death. Nobody can escape My decree!"

Then Gabriel said to God, "Please give this mission to someone else." God then turned to Michael, the angel, asking him to take the soul of Moses.

But Michael too refused to accept the mission.

God then went to the angel Zagzagel, who refused to take Moses' soul since he was Moses' teacher.

Finally, God went to Samael, the Angel of Death, who rejoiced in anticipation of carrying out such a mission.

Samael took his sword and ran to get Moses. When he finally met him, he drew back, because the face of Moses radiated with a bright light.

"What do you want from me?" asked Moses.

"God has asked me to bring back your soul," Samael responded.

"I will not give you my soul," shouted Moses. "Leave at once!"

"All souls were delivered into my hands since the very

creation of the world," responded Samael. "Now let me take yours as well."

"Go away," screamed Moses. "I will not surrender my soul."

In great terror Samael returned to God and said, "I cannot approach the man to whom You sent me."

God was now very angry and again commanded Samael to fetch Moses' soul.

So Samael drew his sword once more. More furious and aroused than ever, Samael returned to Moses. Moses struck him with his staff and blinded him. At that very moment, a ringing voice was heard from heaven saying, "Moses, your last second is at hand."

Hearing this, Moses cried, "O God, do You remember the day You appeared to me at the burning bush and charged me to go to Pharaoh? Do You not also remember the day I ascended into heaven and did not eat or drink for forty days? I pray, O God, do not release me into the hands of the Angel of Death."

Then God spoke again: "Moses, be comforted, for I Myself will take your soul and will personally bury you."

Various traditional sources

How to Enter the
Garden of Eden

Background: This story is another in a series whose theme
is the connection of doing good deeds with attaining a
place in the World to Come.

Once in the town of Koritz there lived a tailor who vio-
lated every *mitzvah* in the Torah. One day he died and the
shammas of the community called upon the townspeople
to attend his funeral. But no one wanted to attend the
funeral of such an evil person. The *gabbai* approached the
home of the learned gaon, Rabbi Pinchas. Surprisingly
the rabbi took his cane and began his walk to the funeral!

When the *gabbai* next visited the gaon, Rabbi Yachba,
and told him that Rabbi Pinchas was attending the tailor's
funeral, the gaon was surprised. Wanting to know why
Rabbi Pinchas would attend, he too decided to go to the
funeral.

When all of the city people saw these two pious rabbis attending the funeral of the sinner, they too became
intrigued and began to follow. Eventually the whole city
turned out at the funeral of the tailor.

On the way home the crowd gathered around Rabbi
Pinchas and asked why he had attended the funeral. Rabbi
Pinchas replied, "Two months ago I was trying to raise
funds for a poor bride. When I finally had succeeded in
raising enough money in order for the ceremony to be
held, the groom backed out. He was promised a new suit
by the bride's parents and unless he received it, he would
call off the wedding.

"In desperation the bride turned to me for help. As I had already approached every resident for a donation, I had no choice but to turn to the tailor for help. That night I entered his home and he gave me a half ruble. But as I was starting to leave, he called me back, saying, 'Rabbi, if I give you the money for the entire suit, will you promise me a place in the World to Come?'

"'Yes,' I said. He then gave me fourteen rubles to purchase the suit, and I was able to perform the wedding. When I heard that this tailor had died, I decided to attend his funeral and see the results of his charitable giving."

"You would not believe it," said the rabbi. "Over his coffin was a shining halo of a suit with angels dancing around the coffin waiting to escort it to Paradise, to the Garden of Eden. Therefore, you can truly see how great is the *mitzvah* of helping a poor bride. One single *mitzvah* alone saved this man and assured him a place in the World to Come."

Various traditional sources

The Death of Rabbi Yochanan ben Zakkai

Background: This story from the Talmud deals with the reason Rabbi Yochanan ben Zakkai cried when he learned of his impending death. The crying resulted from Rabbi Yochanan's not knowing whether the future would bring him to Paradise or *Gehinnom*.

When Rabbi Yochanan ben Zakkai was very ill, his students visited him. Seeing them, Rabbi Yochanan started to weep. "Lamp of Israel, mighty hammer," they said to him. "Why are you crying?"

Rabbi Yochanan answered, "If I were being led today before a human king, whose anger, if he were angry with me, would not be everlasting; whose prison, if he imprisoned me, would not hold me forever; who, if he sentenced me to death, would not sentence me to death eternal; and whom I could persuade with words and bribe with money, even so I would still cry.

"And now I am being led before the Sovereign of Sovereigns, the Holy One, who lives and endures forever. If God is angry with me, God's anger is everlasting. If God imprisons me, God's prison will hold me forever. If God sentences me to die, it is to death eternal. And I cannot persuade God with words or bribe God with money. And furthermore, there are two paths that lie before me. One path leads to Paradise and the other to *Gehinnom*, and I do not know on which path I will be taken. Should I not then weep?"

Babylonian Talmud, *Berachot* 28b

Rabbi Elimelech of Lyzhansk

Background: The prospect of death demands that one tell the truth. This story about Rabbi Elimelech emphasizes the important value of telling the truth, especially within the context of death.

Rabbi Elimelech of Lyzhansk, a chasidic rabbi, once said, "When I die and stand in the court of justice, they will ask me if I have been as just and righteous as I should have been. And I will answer no.

"Then I will be asked if I have been as charitable as I should have been, and I again will answer no.

"Then I will be asked if I studied as much as I should have, and once again I will answer no.

"Then one more time I will be asked if I prayed as much as I should have, and I again will answer no.

"Finally, the Supreme Judge on High will smile and say to me, 'Elimelech, you have spoken the truth. For this alone you will have a share of the World to Come.'"

Folktale

The Martyrdom of Rabbi Hananiah ben Teradyon

Background: This story makes reference to an event that took place during the Hadrianic persecution following the year 135 C.E. During the Roman occupation of Palestine, the leading rabbis of the country continued to meet with colleagues and teach Torah to their students, in defiance of the Roman government. Each was killed for the Sanctification of God's Name. As part of the penitential prayers of the *Musaf*/Additional Service on Yom Kippur, the traditional prayer book includes a martyrology section that records the death of the ten rabbis killed at the hands of the Romans (including Rabbi Hananiah ben Teradyon), all for *Kiddush Hashem*, the Sanctification of God's Name.

Rabbi Hananiah ben Teradyon was found by the Romans studying the Torah, holding public gatherings of his disciples, and keeping a Torah scroll next to his heart. He did all of these things in violation of Roman law.

The Romans then wrapped him in the scroll. Placing wood around him, they set everything on fire. The Romans then brought tufts of wool that had been soaked in water and placed them next to his heart so that he would die even more slowly.

His disciples called to him, "Rabbi, what do you see?"

Rabbi Hananiah answered, "The parchment is being burned but the letters of the Torah are soaring on high."

"Open your mouth so that the fire will penetrate you," they said.

And the rabbi answered, "Let God who gave me my soul take it away, but let no one injure himself."

Babylonian Talmud, *Avodah Zarah* 18a

The Death of Rabban Gamliel

Background: This talmudic story describes the origin of
the custom of treating both rich and poor alike, with equal
respect, according to matters of life and particularly death.

Formerly, they used to bring food to a house of mourning. Rich people were known to always bring baskets of
gold and silver, and poor people brought baskets made of
willow twigs. This made the poorer people feel ashamed.
Then a law was passed that said everyone should use baskets of willow twigs, out of deference to the poor.

There was also a time when they used to serve drinks
in a house of mourning. Rich people would serve their
drinks in white glasses and the poor in less-expensive
colored ones. And once again, the poor felt ashamed. Then
a law was passed that required everyone to serve their
drinks in colored glasses, in deference to the poor.

Formerly they used to bring out the deceased for
burial with the rich on a tall ornamented bed and the poor
in a plain box. When the poor felt ashamed, they enacted
a law that all should be brought out in a plain pine box, in
deference to the poor.

And finally, the expense of burying the dead was even
harder for a family to bear than death itself, so that some
families tried to escape in order to rid themselves of the
expense. This continued to occur until Rabban Gamliel
ordered that he be buried in a plain linen shroud instead
of in expensive garments. And since his time, Jewish people
have been buried in plain white linen shrouds.

Babylonian Talmud, *Mo'ed Katan* 27a–b

The Appearance of Adam

Background: This story, from the foundational book of Jewish mysticism, the *Zohar*, teaches us that we are all responsible for our actions in life. In essence, this story is a polemic against the Christian view of original sin, which posits that all people are born tainted with the sin committed by Adam and Eve in the Garden of Eden.

When a person is about to die, Adam, the first human being, appears to her and asks her why and in what state she leaves the world. The person responds to Adam's inquiry by saying, "Woe to you. Because of you, I have to die."

Adam replies to this statement, "I transgressed one *mitzvah* and was punished for doing so. Look and see how many of God's instructions, both negative and positive, you transgressed."

Adam appears to every person at the moment of that person's departure from life to testify that the person is dying of his or her own sins, and not because of the sin of Adam.

Zohar I

Rabbi Nachman's Death

Background: While some may express their fear of death differently from others, few among us truly want to leave this earth. This talmudic story reflects one particular rabbi's fear of dying.

While seated at the bedside of Rabbi Nachman, Rava watched him as he slipped into death.

Rabbi Nachman said to Rava, "Please tell the Angel of Death not to torture me."

Rava replied, "You are a man of great honor; you may speak directly to the angel."

Nachman answered, "Who is honored, who is distinguished, who is singled out before the Angel of Death?"

As Rabbi Nachman lay dying, Rava said, "Show yourself to me after you die."

Rabbi Nachman died and did appear to Rava in a dream. Rava asked, "Did you suffer much pain?"

Rabbi Nachman answered, "It was as easy as taking a hair from a pitcher of milk. But if God were now to say to me, 'Go back to the world as you were before,' I would not want to go. For the fear of death is very great there."

Babylonian Talmud, *Mo'ed Katan* 28a

The Death of Rabbi

Background: In Jewish tradition, it is generally not acceptable to pray to hasten another's death. Yet this story describes an occasion where one prays for the death of a talmudic sage who was suffering greatly.

On the day that Rabbi was dying, the rabbis proclaimed a public fast and offered prayers for God's divine mercy. They also decreed that whoever said Rabbi had died would be stabbed with a sword.

Rabbi's handmaid climbed to the roof and prayed, "The angels want Rabbi to join them, and the mortals want Rabbi to remain with them; may it be Your will, O God, that the mortals overpower the angels."

However, when the handmaid saw how much Rabbi was suffering, she again prayed, "May it be Your will that the angels overpower the mortals."

As the rabbis continued their prayers for mercy, the handmaid picked up a pitcher and threw it from the roof down to the ground. For a moment they stopped praying, and the soul of Rabbi departed.

Babylonian Talmud, *Ketubot* 104a

The Death of the Rebbe of Rizhyn

Background: In Jewish tradition, when one dies on or close to the Sabbath, it has been considered meritorious. In this chasidic tale, the aged Rabbi Israel of Rizhyn resigns himself to the fact that he will die following the next Sabbath and that his children will take his place.

In his old age, Rabbi Israel of Rizhyn spent his summers in the small town of Potok. One particular day Rabbi Moshe of Kobryn came to visit him for the Sabbath. That day, Rabbi Israel did not eat his meal at the end of the Sabbath but sat in his garden, where the rabbi of Kobryn kept him company.

For a long period of time there was silence between the two men. Finally, Rabbi Israel broke the silence, saying to Rabbi Moshe, "We could eat the fruits of this tree in place of the meal, couldn't we?" Then he touched Rabbi Moshe's shoulder and said, "Let's take a short walk."

As they began to walk, Rabbi Israel repeated what he had said before. "Rabbi Moshe, you are a learned man. Is it not true that we are permitted to replace the meal at the close of the Sabbath with fruits?"

It was then that Rabbi Moshe finally understood that Rabbi Israel was speaking of his own death and of his sons. He cried out, "Our holy rabbi, the world still needs you!" But a month and a half after this particular Sabbath, Rabbi Israel died.

Chasidic tale

Learning How to Die

Background: Some people die suddenly and do not have the opportunity to prepare for their deaths. Thus, we are taught to spend our lives in *teshuvah*, always ready for death. Others are aware of impending death and can thus prepare for it. In this chasidic story, Rabbi Abraham Moshe teaches us that before one can make preparations for death, one must learn "how" to do it.

One Chanukah, when Rabbi Abraham Moshe found himself in the city of Biala with his mother, he said to her, "Mother, I have a real desire to die." She answered, "I heard from your father that first a person has to learn how to die." He answered, "Mother, I have indeed learned it!"

Again she repeated, "I have heard from your father that a person has to learn for a very long time, and to learn it properly." Rabbi Moshe answered, "I have learned long enough," and lay down. He died on the seventh day of Chanukah. Afterward, his mother discovered that her son had visited his favorite disciples and taken leave of them.

Chasidic tale

The Death of the Baal Shem Tov

Background: The Baal Shem Tov, the Master of the Good Name, was the founder of the chasidic movement. Many stories are attributed to him. In this story, we learn that one of the most significant acts of kindness concerns caring for the dead. With that *mitzvah* alone, which the tradition refers to as *chesed v'emet* (one of true loving-kindness), there is no possibility that one performs the *mitzvah* in anticipation that the "*mitzvah* doer" will receive a reward from the person who benefits from the *mitzvah*.

The Baal Shem Tov had become very ill. In the days prior to his death, he would sit alone in his room just so he might think about his life. Each day his body grew weaker and his voice became more faint.

On the eve of Shavuot, the very last of his life, his friends gathered around him and he taught them about the giving of the Torah on Mount Sinai. Subsequently, he requested all his disciples to gather together in his room in order to teach them how to care for his body following his death. Afterward, the Baal Shem Tov asked for a prayer book and said, "I wish to spend a little while more with the Master on High."

Shortly thereafter, his disciples heard him talking to someone and they asked him to whom he was speaking. The Baal Shem Tov replied, "Don't you see the Angel of Death? He always flees from me, but now his wings flutter and he is filled with joy."

Later, all the people of the city gathered together to greet the Baal Shem Tov on the eve of Shavuot, and he spoke words of Torah to them. Then he said, "Until now I have treated you with loving acts of kindness. Now you must treat me the same way."

He then gave his disciples a sign that at his death the two clocks in the house would stop. While he was washing his hands, the large clock stopped and some of his disciples stood in front of it so that the others would not see it. He said to them, "I'm not worried about myself, for I am certain that I will go from this door and immediately enter another door."

The Baal Shem Tov then sat down on his bed and told his students to gather around him. He spoke words of Torah and ordered them to recite the verse "And let Your graciousness, O God, be upon us. Establish also the work of our hands."

With these words, the Baal Shem Tov lay down and prayed with the greatest of devotion. He told his students to cover him with blankets. He began to shake and tremble as he was in the habit of doing when he prayed the Silent Prayer. Slowly, little by little, he became still. At the very moment that the small clock stopped, they realized that the Baal Shem Tov had died. It was Shavuot, 1760.

Chasidic tale

Reward in the World to Come

Background: The rabbis introduced the notion of a reward in the World to Come to Judaism as part of the oral tradition that they taught. This story from the midrash emphasizes this rabbinic teaching, stressing the fact that a person will be rewarded for his or her study of the Torah not in this world but in the future World to Come.

Once a student of Rabbi Simeon ben Yochai left the land of Israel and came back a wealthy man. When the other students saw him, they were extremely jealous and wished that they too might travel abroad. When Rabbi Simeon learned of this envy, he brought all of his students to a valley near the village of Meron, where he began to pray, "O valley, fill up with gold dinars!"

Immediately, before his very eyes, the entire valley began to give forth a stream of golden coins. He then said to his students, "If it is gold that you want, here is your gold. Take it now. But you should know that the one who takes it now is taking one's share of the World to Come, since the reward for studying Torah is not in this world. Rather, it is in the World to Come."

Exodus Rabbah 52:3 and Yalkut, *Proverbs* 964

The Death of
Rabbi Meir's Children

Background: This story from the midrash is a tale about
the two sons of Rabbi Meir who died on the Sabbath at
home while their father was in the synagogue. Rabbi Meir's
wise wife, Beruriah, one of the few women in the Talmud
cited for her own wisdom, was home at the time. The rabbis relate this painful story because they are interested in
determining how to handle such a difficult situation,
especially since Jewish law expressly forbids mourning on
the holy Sabbath. This tale is given as a commentary on
Proverbs 31:10: "A woman of valor, who can find?"

One Sabbath afternoon, when Rabbi Meir had returned
to the synagogue to study, his two sons fell violently ill
and died. Their mother, Beruriah, was overcome with grief.
But what could she do? The Sabbath was a day of joy. All
of the laws of mourning are suspended on Shabbat! She
carried the two boys into her bedroom and covered them.
In the evening, Rabbi Meir returned home from the House
of Study. "Where are the children?" he asked. "I missed
them at the synagogue."

Instead of answering the question, Beruriah handed
him a cup of wine so that he could make *Havdalah* and
usher out the Sabbath from their midst. After reciting the
prayers of *Havdalah*, Rabbi Meir again asked his wife,
"Where are the two boys?"

She replied, "Sometimes they go someplace, and now
they're on their way." She then placed the evening meal
before him and they both ate.

After reciting the blessing after the meal she said to him, "I would like to ask you a question."

He told her, "Ask your question."

She said, "A short time ago some precious jewels were entrusted to my care. I became so attached to them that I regarded them as if they were my own. Now, the true owner has come to take them back. Shall we return them or not?"

He replied, "I am very surprised that you do not know the law and you would ask me such a question. Naturally the jewels belong to their owner and must be returned!"

She responded, "I wouldn't have returned them without your consent." Beruriah then gently led her husband by the hand to the room and slowly lifted the sheet from the bodies of their dead sons.

He began to cry and shouted, "My sons, my sons!"

Tearfully she reminded him, "Did you not say that we must return to the rightful Owner that which has been entrusted to us? Our sons were the jewels that God left with us." Together they wept, and they said, "God has given and God has now taken away. Blessed is the righteous Judge."

Proverbs Rabbah 31:10; *Yalkut,* Proverbs 964

The Butcher
Who Entered Paradise

Background: This story emphasizes a theme that recurs
often in Jewish literature. One should fulfill all outstanding debts before one can enter the World to Come with
peace of mind.

Once upon a time in the city of Koznitz there lived a
butcher named Isaac. Since Isaac died at a very young age,
there were many rumors about how badly he behaved in
his youth.

Weeks after his death, he appeared in a dream before
the *shochet* (the one who performed ritual slaughter) and
summoned the slaughterer to a *bet din* (rabbinic court).

The slaughterer was very frightened by this dream.
However, since it was only a dream, he paid very little attention to it. But the dream recurred a second and a third
night!

Now the *shochet* was extremely frightened and went
to the Koznitzer Maggid to ask for advice. He was advised
that the Torah is not in the heavens and that should the
dead man bother him again, he should tell him to appear
back on earth before the judgment of the Koznitzer rabbi.

The following night, the butcher again appeared in a
dream, and the *shochet* shared with him the words of the
rabbi. The butcher agreed to appear before the judgment
of the Koznitzer rabbi.

That morning the *shochet* related all that had happened to the Koznitzer. The rabbi ordered that a partition
of wooden boards be built in his study and that his ser-

vant be sent to the cemetery to summon the dead butcher to appear.

Several minutes later, the voice of the butcher was heard from behind the partition. He was crying that the *shochet* had made many of his cattle nonkosher. Because of this, he had become very poor and had been in severe debt. The cattle had been purchased with borrowed money. He had lost everything and died before his time. Now the creditors were haunting his wife and demanding full payment. She did not have any money and they were threatening to take her home away from her.

Now, in the World of Truth, he had discovered that all of the cattle that had been previously called nonkosher were indeed kosher. The *shochet* had only taken advantage of him because of a grudge. Because of this he could not find peace of mind. He did not want his wife frightened and his children to go hungry. These were his charges.

When the *shochet* heard this he was very frightened. Admitting his guilt, he asked the rabbi to punish him. The rabbi ordered the *shochet* to make good on all of the butcher's debts and to provide the widow with a weekly allowance. The *shochet* immediately accepted the judgment.

After leaving the rabbi's study, the rabbi pointed his finger toward the dead butcher and said, "Isaac, come here. I am very surprised that immediately after your death you have nothing on your mind except for a lawsuit against the *shochet*. Have you no other worries? Have you no other accounts to settle in the heavens?"

"Your questions are in order," replied the butcher. "Allow me to explain. When I was a young boy, I was a coachman and drove from city to city. Once a group of *tzadikim* were in my coach. On the road we were overtaken by a group of bandits who wanted to kill all of my passengers. I fought them off, even though my own life was in danger. God was surely on my side.

"When I died and reached the Other World, groups of evil angels met me and were ready to throw me into the shadow of hell. In a few moments righteous people appeared, the same ones whom I saved while I was a coachman. They said to the bad angels, 'We will not allow you to harm him, for he saved all of us from death. We have been taught that the person who saves even one life saves an entire world. Because of him we were able to continue to study Torah and perform deeds of kindness. He has a share in the Torah that we learned and in all the good deeds that we performed in the world below,' they said before the heavenly court.

"And so it happened that I was saved from being sent to hell. Nevertheless, I could not enter Paradise until I had cleared my earthly accounts, for sins committed between people can be forgiven only when all debts are paid. Then I discovered that the *shochet* had caused all of my troubles. Now that he has pledged to do justly by paying back all of my debts and providing for my family, I will be able to return in peace to my place in the World to Come."

Chasidic story

Rabbi Shimon ben Halafta Confronts the Angel of Death

Background: Even in the midst of celebration, we reflect on our own finitude. Some may consider it morbid, but such an approach reflects the reality of mortal living. In this story, Rabbi Shimon ben Halafta confronts the Angel of Death on his return home from a celebration following the *brit milah* of a member of his community.

Once Rabbi Shimon ben Halafta went to a celebration following a *brit milah* (a *seudah mitzvah*). The boy's parents sponsored the banquet and offered their guests seven-year-old wine to drink. They said to their guests, "We will set aside some of this wine for the wedding feast of our son." The celebration continued until midnight. Rabbi Shimon ben Halafta, who trusted in his power to fight off demons, left the party at midnight in order to return home.

On his way home, he encountered the Angel of Death but saw something peculiar about it. So he said, "Who are you?" The angel answered, "I am God's messenger." So Rabbi Shimon said, "Why do you refer to yourself that way?" The angel replied, "Because of the way people talk. They say, 'We shall do this and this,' and they do not know when they will be called to die. Those people who just celebrated the *brit milah* of their child, their turn will come in thirty days."

Rabbi Shimon said, "Show me my turn." But the angel replied, "I have no power over you and those like you

252

because the Holy One wants your good deeds and length-
ens your [and their] lives."

Based on *Deuteronomy Rabbah* 9:1

The Seven Stages of Life

Background: This midrashic story provides us a window of insight into the rabbinic mind as it searches for descriptions of various stages in the life of a person. It serves as a fitting conclusion for our collection of stories from the Jewish life cycle.

When a person is a year old, that person is like a king. Everybody loves and embraces him. At two, that person is like a pig, wallowing in the dirt. During his childhood, that person is like a kid, dancing and laughing all day. When a person is eighteen years of age, he is like a horse, rejoicing in his youth and strength. When a person marries, that person is like a donkey, carrying its burden. Later on in life, a person becomes like a dog, unashamed to ask for favors and beg for a livelihood. In a person's old age, he is like a monkey who is curious and childish, with no one paying any attention to his words.

Tanhuma, *Pekudei*